STEP BY STEP:
A PROGRAM FOR CHILDREN AND FAMILIES

# CREATING CHILD-CENTERED PROGRAMS FOR INFANTS AND TODDLERS

ELEANOR STOKES SZANTON, EDITOR
FOREWORD BY PAMELA A. COUGHLIN

CHILDREN'S RESOURCES INTERNATIONAL, INC.
WASHINGTON, DC

Library of Congress Card Number: 00-103991

Children's Resources International, a nonprofit organization located in Washington, DC, promotes the implementation of sound educational practices developed in the United States while maintaining the cultural traditions of the participating countries.

The Soros Foundations/Open Society Institute is a network of foundations, programs, and institutions established and supported by philanthropist George Soros to foster the development of Open Societies around the world, particularly in the former communist countries of Central and Eastern Europe and the former Soviet Union. To this end, the Soros Foundation cooperates with Children's Resources International to develop and implement the project called *Step by Step: A Program for Children and Families.*

Children's Resources International, Inc.
5039 Connecticut Ave., NW, Suite One
Washington, DC 20008
202.363.9002 *phone*
202.363.9550 *fax*
*E-Mail:* info@crinter.com

Open Society Institute, New York
400 West 59th Street
New York, New York 10019
212.548.0600 *phone*
212.548.4679 *fax*
*E-Mail*: osnews@sorosny.org

# FOREWORD

In 1994, the Open Society Institute, Soros Foundations, and Children's Resources International formed a partnership to introduce child-centered teaching methods to the well-established education systems in Eastern and Central Europe and the countries of the former Soviet Union. The aim was to engender democratic ideals and principles within young children. Step by Step, the educational program that grew out of this partnership, encourages children to think critically and to make choices and understand the consequences of these choices. The program promotes children's creativity, individualized learning, and resourcefulness. It alters the role of the teacher from providing information to facilitating learning. Family involvement in children's education is the cornerstone of the Step by Step Program.

*Creating Child-Centered Programs for Infants and Toddlers* is part of a series developed for caregivers and teachers in early childhood programs. Initially directed at the preschool level for children ages three to five years, the series was extended at the request of parents and teachers who have seen children flourish in child-centered classrooms. This manual brings the child-centered approach to programs for infants and toddlers.

Caregivers who work with infants and toddlers in group settings have a tremendous responsibility. More growth and development takes place in the first three years than at any other time in a child's life. Researchers confirm what has been known for centuries: young children thrive when they have a chance to develop secure attachments to significant adults in their lives.

*Creating Child-Centered Programs for Infants and Toddlers* draws on the infant's natural interest and urge to learn and his need for close, responsive relationships with caregivers. Designed for ease of application, the manual offers caregivers practical advice on how to support infants' and toddlers' emotional, social, cognitive, language, and physical development; recognize and respond to each child's temperament and interests; create an environment that is safe, healthy, and stimulating; and work with families and other professionals to ensure a quality program.

*Creating Child-Centered Programs for Infants and Toddlers,* developed by U.S. experts in the field of early childhood development, is based on sound theoretical principles and proven practices. The educators who have successfully implemented Step by Step over the past several years guided the manual's development from conception through birth. Our hope is that its application helps the youngest citizens get off to a strong and healthy start.

Pam Coughlin
Children's Resources International

# TABLE OF CONTENTS

* Indicates a chart, form, or checklist.

# ACKNOWLEDGEMENTS

George Soros' abiding commitment to open societies and belief that even the youngest members of these societies can practice basic democratic freedoms has been the motivation for the development of this book and others in the series, *Creating Child-Centered Classrooms*.

The staff at CRI is deeply grateful to Liz Lorant and Sarah Klaus at the Open Society Institute for providing the direction and resources that have allowed the Step by Step Program to develop and flourish in the emerging democracies where Soros Foundations operate on four continents. Their assistance and encouragement continues to be an invaluable source of support for us.

The staff of the country teams working in closest proximity to the children and families were the first to recognize the need to extend the philosophy of the Step by Step Program to infants and toddlers. They requested the development of this publication and will implement its concepts. We are at once humbled and inspired by their dedication to creating an educational experience of both excellence and personal freedom for children and families; in the process they are reshaping their societies.

A team of many contributors collaborated to produce *Creating Child-Centered Programs for Infants and Toddlers* and we are most thankful to them. Eleanor Stokes Szanton edited the publication to ensure its theoretical and practical soundness. Thanks to Michele Redalen and Georgiana McGuire, who edited the many voices of the contributors with unfailing good humor. Jean Iker enlivens the text with her joyful illustrations, experience of teaching very young children, and newfound pleasure as grandmother to Sarah. Jamie duPont, our photographer, has captured excellent examples of committed caregivers in group settings. The staff of Broadcasters' Child Development Center, Smithsonian Early Enrichment Center, and Step by Step Programs in Slovenia and Macedonia opened their programs for us to capture through photographs. Thanks to The Crosby Group's design of the cover which captures both the whimsy and promise of the early years.

Each of the staff at CRI contributed to make the publication a better one. Pam Coughlin, Julie Empson, and Carolyn Rutsch have reviewed and critiqued the many drafts. Cassie Marshall laid out and produced a document that is both pleasing to look at and easy to read. We hope you enjoy it.

The Staff of Children's Resources International, Inc.

# PART I

# INTRODUCTION

# CHAPTER 1

# INTRODUCTION, PROGRAM RATIONALE, AND PHILOSOPHY

# 1. INTRODUCTION, PROGRAM RATIONALE, AND PHILOSOPHY

Step by Step is a program for children and their families. This manual guides caregivers through the very first steps of the care and education of the youngest children. This introductory chapter provides the context for understanding the research and practical strategies in the chapters that follow. It gives an overview of the Step by Step Program and the philosophical principles on which the program is built, and provides a description of the infant and toddler program that is discussed in detail throughout the manual.

## Overview of the Step by Step Program

Throughout their lives, regardless of where they live, today's children will have to face change: social, political, environmental, scientific, technological, and industrial. The rapid changes occurring throughout the world today make it important to nurture in children a desire for lifelong learning. The Step by Step Program maintains that lifelong learning as a preparation for change occurs most effectively when guided by the principles of democracy. In order to prepare children to be lifelong learners in democratic societies, the Step by Step Program builds a foundation for the attitudes, knowledge, and skills that will be needed in rapidly changing times. Among these are the ability to:

- Think critically
- Make choices
- Identify and solve problems
- Care about individuals, community, country, and environment
- Be creative, imaginative, and resourceful

The program integrates research-based practices of early childhood education with a firm commitment to work with families and communities to meet each child's particular needs. The program is designed to respect a variety of cultural traditions. Even for the very youngest children, all Step by Step learning environments share three characteristics:

- Individualized learning experiences
- Emphasis on learning through play and making choices
- Family participation

## *Philosophy of the Step by Step Program*

The Step by Step Program is based on the belief that children grow best when they are involved with their own learning. The learning environment encourages children to explore, initiate, and create, and the teaching team has a sound knowledge of child development.

The teaching team creates the environment and provides the materials for learning. The team's role is to set appropriate goals for individual children and for the group as a whole, respond to the interests of the children, respect the individual strengths and needs of each child, and nourish the natural curiosity of the young child.

## Theoretical Foundations of the Step by Step Program

The Step by Step Program encompasses the major early childhood educational theories of constructivism and developmentally appropriate practice.

### *Constructivism*

Constructivists believe that learning occurs as children strive to make sense of the world around them. Children construct or build their own understanding of the world. They make sense of what is happening around them by synthesizing new experiences with what they have previously come to understand. Learning becomes an interactive process involving the child, adults, other children, and the environment. Jacqueline and Martin Brooks (1993) described the process in this way:

> *Often we encounter an object, an idea, a relationship or a phenomenon that doesn't quite make sense to us. When confronted with such initially discrepant data or perceptions, we either interpret what we see to conform to our present set of rules for explaining and ordering our world or we generate a new set of rules that better accounts for what we perceive to be occurring. Either way, our perceptions and rules are constantly engaged in a grand dance that shapes our understandings.*

The following example illustrates constructivist learning. A young child whose family has a dog is out driving with his parents. As they pass a cow in a field, the child points and says "dog." His parents tell him that it is a cow and explain how a cow is different from a dog, although they are both animals. The new information will be refigured against what is known and mental accommodations will be made. Although children must construct their own understanding and knowledge, the role of adult as facilitator and mediator is essential. The teaching team must provide the tools, materials, support, guidance, and interest to maximize the child's opportunities for learning.

### Developmentally Appropriate Practice

A developmentally appropriate curriculum is one that is based on a knowledge of child development: the understanding that all children progress through common developmental stages and, at the same time, that each child is a unique and individual being. The teaching team must know about typical child growth and development in order to provide a realistic array of learning materials and activities. The team must also watch and listen for differences between the skills and special interests of same-age children (Seefeldt and Barbour, 1994; Bredekamp and Copple, 1997). A developmentally appropriate curriculum includes activities that are based on children's interests, their cognitive level of functioning, and their social and emotional maturity. Such activities appeal to young children's natural curiosity, enjoyment of sensory experiences, and the desire to explore their own ideas.

A developmentally appropriate program is designed to help children answer their own questions. When children pose the questions, their interest, motivation, and attention are automatic. The teacher's role is to find ways to arrive at answers that satisfy the child without oversimplifying the question or overwhelming the child with information. Through developmentally appropriate practices, teachers can find a balance that satisfies and extends each learning situation.

## Characteristics of the Step by Step Program

### Individualizing the Learning Experience

The Step by Step environment is a dynamic and changing one filled with materials and experiences designed to correspond to children's individual interests and developmental stages. The Step by Step teaching teams set the foundation for children to become fulfilled, achieving, active adults who will care about others and have an impact on their world. At the same time, the teachers are also concerned with the "here and now" of childhood. They implement this dual focus by valuing play and individualized learning.

Each child has a unique pattern and timing of growth, as well as an individual temperament, learning style, and family background. Both the curriculum and adults' interactions with children should be responsive to those individual differences. Learning in young children is the result of interactions between the child's thoughts and experiences with materials, ideas, and people. These experiences should match the child's developing abilities while challenging the child's interest and understanding (Bredekamp and Copple, 1997).

Why is it important to individualize the learning experience? When the experience is individualized, the child can grow and develop at his own pace. Individualizing matches the learning activity with the developmental stage, strengths, interests, and needs of each child. When this match occurs, children succeed in their activities. They gain competence and self-esteem. They become confident and ready to tackle new challenges.

A child-centered environment supports individualized learning. It is a dynamic and changing environment, filled with materials and experiences designed to correspond to children's individual interests and developmental stages. The equipment, materials, and layout of the classroom enhance the growth of every child. Children individualize for themselves when they choose an activity or select a ball rather than a teddy bear.

Individualization also requires that the teacher create activities that make each child feel successful and challenged. By planning flexible and interesting activities and by carefully observing children during their routine activities and play, the teacher can change and adapt materials and activities as needed.

## Learning Through Play and Making Choices

Play is the heart of good early childhood programs. The research on play shows that it is an important part of the lives of young children (Johnson, Christie, Yawkey, 1987). Play and development unfold together, so environments for young children must provide ongoing opportunities for free play. Play occurs in a wide variety of ways: solitary play with objects; unstructured, associative play with one other child; interactive and complex dramatic play with props and other children; and more structured play in group games as children get older.

Experts maintain that:

> *Children need to play in order to develop cognitive and motor skills and to learn about the social world and their place in it. Children develop social skills through*

*interaction with their peers. They learn what rules are, how rules are made and what justice and fairness are about. They learn how to cooperate and how to share. They develop self-esteem by successfully challenging themselves, by interacting with other children and by mastering personal, physical, intellectual and social challenges* (Frost and Jacobs, 1995, p. 47).

Opportunities to develop these skills through play should be offered to children from the earliest years.

Children learn best when they have an opportunity to create their own knowledge from their experiences and their interactions with the world around them. The materials in the classroom should stimulate and challenge children to use all their senses. Through experimentation, investigation, and discovery, children test ideas and gain information in their own individual ways. This is how children begin to develop the habit of finding and solving problems, thinking critically, making choices, and developing concepts.

The role of the caregiving team is to act as facilitators. They are ready to extend and enhance play by knowing when to ask open-ended questions that encourage thinking. They know when to provide appropriate information, when to clarify misconceptions, when to add materials, and, if feasible, when to arrange new experiences such as short trips, that will further stimulate the children's interests and learning. It is a basic belief of the Step by Step Program that teachers who themselves model playfulness are most likely to appreciate the importance of an environment that provides opportunities and times for play.

## Staffing Practices

In order to implement all features of the Step by Step philosophy—developmentally appropriate practice, individualized learning, learning through play and choice, and family involvement—and to ensure a consistently high quality of care, all Step by Step programs incorporate four fundamental staffing practices:

- **Training** The staff should have both theoretical and practical preparation in early childhood education as well as continued training to enhance professional development.
- **Continuity of care** Each child must have one primary caregiver whose attachment provides the emotional foundation for learning. The same person cares for the child from infancy through age three to give the child an uninterrupted learning experience.

- ***Low child/staff ratio*** The demands of the routine activities for infants and toddlers, combined with the necessity of individualized learning, require a low ratio of children to staff. Though the experts disagree on the exact numbers, Head Start Performance Standards require a ratio of four children to one caregiver for infants and toddlers. Others argue a smaller ratio for infants (birth to 18 months) is ideal, no more than three infants to one caregiver.
- ***Group size*** Very young children are most comfortable among very small numbers of people. Here again, the experts disagree on the exact numbers. Head Start programs limit group size of infants and toddlers to no more than eight children. Others argue that the group size of very young infants (from birth to 8 months) should be limited to six infants, mobile infants (ages 8 to 18 months) no more than nine, and toddlers (ages 18 to 36 months) may have up to 12 children in a group. Please follow the guidelines establised by your state or local childcare agency.

## Family Participation

Family participation is integral to the Step by Step Program. Step by Step recognizes that families have the greatest influence on their children. For infants and toddlers, family participation is especially important, because the bond of attachment that exists between the baby and parents extends to the caregiver and is the prerequisite for all learning.

Families are their children's primary educators. Families want the best for their children and want them to be successful and productive citizens. Therefore, Step by Step caregivers and administrators encourage all families to become involved in all aspects of the program and build parent participation activities into the program. Although methods of involving families vary from program to program and family to family, depending on individual and community circumstances, the operating principle is that all families are welcomed and invited to participate in many ways.

Parents and caregivers share information about the activities of the children both at home and at the program. Each program has a Family Room that offers comfortable surroundings, information about the program and child development, books and other reading materials of interest to families, snacks, and space for activities or conversation. Families are welcomed as program volunteers. They serve in a formal advisory capacity through the Family Advisory Committee. They are encouraged to borrow toys and educational materials through a lending library.

In summary, the Step by Step Program's goal is to build a supportive community that holds the family at the center and includes the teaching team and community members. This group of people creates a network that plans, discusses, and communicates issues and concerns in order to build a program that nurtures and supports the growth and development of children and their families.

## *Child-Centered Environment*

A child-centered environment is based on two core principles:

- Children create their own knowledge from their experiences and interactions with the world around them.
- Caregivers foster children's growth and development best by building on the interests, needs, and strengths of the children.

Teachers are responsible for transforming the environment into a kind of laboratory where children experiment with roles as explorers, artists, friends, and scientists. They are responsible for organizing materials to encourage children's creative and ongoing experimentation, discovery, and problem solving.

Teachers respect children's ideas and use those ideas to mold the curriculum. Teachers interact with children as they work and play: they model supportive, caring behaviors; they observe and listen; they record and evaluate their observations; and they use their observations in planning and individualizing for children. In an environment where teachers encourage children to pursue their interests, children develop a strong sense of importance and self-initiative.

Teachers set the mood and tone for the learning environment. They personify the qualities that they want to help develop in the children—empathy, caring, enthusiasm, and intellectual curiosity. They should also remember how to have fun. Few things are more rewarding than the joy expressed by a child who has joined a teacher to blow bubbles or talk about a new interest. Teachers who communicate their enthusiasm to children make learning exciting and vital. Teachers who are aloof and authoritarian may frighten children and inhibit their curiosity.

In a child-centered environment, both children and teachers initiate and direct activities. A delicate balance is achieved, with each participant taking turns leading, inquiring, and responding. Children are encouraged to initiate much of their own learning; their creative expression is promoted and valued. The teacher takes advantage of the interests and activities of the children and uses them to stimulate further thinking and learning. By providing opportunities for children to have direct contact with people, materials, and real-life experiences, the teacher fosters each child's intellectual growth.

11

## *Step by Step Infant and Toddler Methodology*

### The Purpose

The Step by Step methodology for infants and toddlers teaches caregivers about the emotional, social, cognitive, language, and physical development of very young children. It encourages caregivers to listen to, guide, and help individual children to make sense of the world around them. It shows the caregivers how to create learning environments that are warm and inviting places as well as clean and safe ones. The methodology reinforces the need to establish a relationship of love, trust, and respect between caregiver and child.

### Infant and Toddler Stages

Throughout this manual, infants and toddlers are described in terms of three categories:

- Young infants (the early months)    Birth through 8 months
- Mobile infants (crawlers and walkers)    8 to 18 months
- Toddlers    18 to 36 months

In general, all references to developmentally appropriate education and care are divided into these categories.

### Terminology

Individuals who work with groups of infants and toddlers have several titles. They are certainly "teachers" as they facilitate learning. They are "caregivers," with emphasis on both the emotional bond between adult and child and the physical demands (feeding, diapering, etc.) of serving very young children. The word "staff" is very general and emphasizes the relationship to the program rather than the children. Throughout this publication, all three terms are used interchangeably since adults fill all three roles when they work with children. Similarly, "she" and "he," "him" and "her" are used interchangeably when referring to children.

## Organization of the Methodology

This manual is divided into five sections:

- Part I, *Introduction*, which includes Chapter 1.

- Part II, *The Research Base for the Methodology*. Chapters 2 and 3 describe the research basis for the new understanding about the importance of the period from birth through three years and the many ways caregivers can support our children's development. These two chapters integrate research with many practical illustrations.

- Part III, *How Infants and Toddlers Learn*. Chapters 4 through 11 together form a child-centered curriculum for working with groups of infants and toddlers.

- Part IV, *The Environment for Learning*, Chapters 12 through 15 discuss health, safety, nutrition, and the design of responsive environments.

- Part V, *Program Staffing and Evaluation*. Chapter 16 delineates basic principles about the organization and evaluation of group care. Individual programs will implement the principles according to their own situations and resources.

- References

- Appendices
  √ Appendix A: Developmental Milestones of Children from Birth to Age 3
  √ Appendix B: Conversion Chart
  √ Appendix C: Recommended Childhood Immunization Schedule Notes

# PART II

# THE RESEARCH BASE FOR THE METHODOLOGY

# CHAPTER 2

# INFANT AND TODDLER DEVELOPMENT

# 2. INFANT AND TODDLER DEVELOPMENT

Over the past 30 years, there has been an enormous increase in what we know about the development of very young children. Much has been learned about what infants can do in the earliest days and weeks of life, and just how competent they already are at that age. Even in the first months, infants are sensitive to factors in their environment. Their development can be greatly influenced, depending on the kind of care they receive and its effects on their individual temperaments. From birth onward they are social and emotional creatures, already learning about the world around them, beginning to feel it is benign and supportive, or that it is frustrating, unloving, and frightening.

This chapter gives an overview of some of the most important new findings from scientific research about the competencies and vulnerabilities of infants and toddlers. It covers (1) prenatal development; (2) brain development; (3) the effects of good nutrition and breast feeding; (4) sensori-motor development; (5) the development of language; (6) the growth of attachment; (7) the interrelatedness of areas of development; (8) the growing sense of self; (9) individual differences in children's temperament; and (10) the significance of cultural diversity.

## Prenatal Development

Because children are greatly affected by their environment even *before* they are born, caregivers must have a basic understanding of the latest research in prenatal development. They will be able to share information with parents who are or will be pregnant again and they will be more aware of possible causes of problems they see in some of the children they care for.

We know that a child, well nourished *in utero,* is born with as many as 100 billion nerve cells, or *neurons,* allowing for the possibility of as many connections between them as there are stars in the universe (National Academy of Sciences, 1995)! Since no neurons are created *after* birth, these are the only neurons the child will ever have. The child has been continuously exposed to his mother's language as its sounds and rhythms travel down her spinal column. Thus the newborn can already discriminate among certain sounds and already prefers the sound of his mother's voice over those of strangers (Jusczyk, P. et al., 1993).

Medical research has confirmed that a mother's balanced, nutritious diet during pregnancy has positive and lasting effects on the development of the fetus, particularly the development of the brain (Rizzo et al., 1997). An increasing body of evidence also demonstrates harmful effects to the fetus if the mother smokes, uses drugs, consumes alcohol, or is exposed to lead while she is pregnant or nursing (Needleman et al., 1990; Olson et al., 1992; Chasnoff et al., 1992; Zuckerman and Brown, 1993; Mayes et al., 1996;

Steissguth et al., 1989; Alliance to End Childhood Lead Poisoning, 2000). Children born to parents who smoke have lower birth weights and lower cognitive competence, on the average, than children of parents who don't smoke. Cocaine and heroin have a negative effect on later competence and are also associated with behavioral problems, such as Attention Deficit Disorder, that interfere with learning. Fetal alcohol syndrome (FAS), one of the most thoroughly studied effects of toxicity *in utero*, alters facial characteristics and is accompanied by mental retardation. For every child diagnosed as an FAS baby, there are many, many more who are less noticeably, but still significantly, affected for life. Similarly, at very high levels of exposure, lead poisoning can cause mental retardation, coma, convulsions, and even death. However, more commonly children are poisoned through low-level exposure to lead dust or paint chips from lead-based paint which can result in a range of disabilities and other health effects. The most tragic aspect of all these conditions is that *they are preventable.*

Still other research suggests that severe maternal emotional stress during pregnancy diminishes fetal neurobehavioral development. The mother's secretion of cortisol, a stress hormone, is transmitted to the fetus and interferes with brain development (Di Pietro, 1997).

## Brain Development During the Early Years

Researchers have also made great advances understanding brain development during infancy. Because human beings are born before their central nervous systems are fully developed, their neurological maturation is susceptible to environmental influences after birth (Greenough, 1987).

### How the Brain Is 'Wired'

From birth until eight months of age, 950 trillion new connections, or *synapses*, are made among the 100 billion brain cells, or *neurons*, present at birth (Huttenlocher, 1994). During this period, the brain becomes an extremely efficient learning machine, thanks to three crucial processes: the myelination of the nerve cells, the channeling or "pruning" of the brain, and the organization of the synaptic connections through which electrical impulses travel.

The myelination of the nerve cells is extremely important because the myelene sheathe insulates the nerves and increases the rate of speed at which electrical impulses travel from neuron to neuron, thereby connecting one part of the brain to another.

New technology (positron emission tomography, or PET, and magnetic resonance imaging, or MRI) has made it possible to watch the brain at work and see which parts are activated in connection with what kinds of behavior and how these parts are electrically connected to each other (Chugani et al., 1987). The research made possible by this technology shows two processes occurring during these earliest months. The brain undergoes an immense channeling or pruning process, discarding useless connections and reinforcing useful connections (Huttenlocher, 1994). At the same time, the synaptic connections become much better organized.

An illustration of the efficiency of the pruning process is seen in the Japanese child who, at three months, has the ability to distinguish between an "r" and an "l" among several hundred sounds. Some months later, the baby is no longer able to distinguish these particular sounds as easily, since the distinction between "r" and "l" is not made in Japanese.

As a child learns more and more about her environment, she begins to lay down orderly *patterns of connections* within the brain. These connections are *not* made if they have no meaning to the child. They *are* made if they build upon previous understanding. We all recognize the phenomenon of learning about a person for the first time and then hearing about him repeatedly over the next few days. A connection is being made that our brain can build upon. In the same way, as the neuronal connections are pruned from 950 to 500 trillion, the child's brain becomes efficient in its ability to understand and respond to the world around him. Teachers and caregivers have a strong role to play in providing the kind of organized, understandable environment that helps build an efficiently functioning brain.

## The Chemistry of the Brain

Recent research has also led to increased knowledge about the chemistry of the brain, including how chemicals enhance or interfere with synaptic transmission of information from neuron to neuron. Children with high levels of chronic anxiety regularly secrete high amounts of the stress hormone cortisol, which impairs their cognitive capacities as well as their immune systems (McEwen et al., 1992; Gunnar et al., 1996). Thus, children who experience extremely high levels of stress at a very early age may be damaged intellectually as well as emotionally. This is particularly true when there is an absence of a secure relationship (Nachmias et al., 1996; Gunnar et al., 1996).

## *The Effects of a Nutritious Diet and Breast-feeding*

A young child's healthy brain development is crucially dependent on a healthy, balanced diet. In the past, protein was believed to be the nutritional key to sound development. Recently, some researchers have come to believe that certain micronutrients—iron, iodine, and zinc—are also extremely important to the brain's healthy development (Pollitt et al., 1996). It has long been established that undernutrition of the fetus has a direct negative effect on later cognitive development. We now know that undernutrition leads to lethargy, hampering a young child's interest in the world around him.

21

Furthermore, a child who does not show interest in his environment is less likely to have interaction with the adults in his life. This, in turn, has a cumulative negative effect on cognitive development (Espinosa et al., 1992).

Poor nutrition also lowers young children's resistance to sickness and disease (Chen, 1983). However, breast-feeding protects babies from disease, because their mothers' antibodies are transferred in the milk. It also appears to lower the risk of chronic disease (Cunningham et al., 1991). Breast milk is also strongly associated with successful development. One recent study showed that premature babies who were tube-fed breast milk scored higher on developmental tests than premature babies who were tube-fed formula (Lucas, 1992). (Other studies that show a strong correlation between breast-feeding and positive developmental outcomes indicate that various factors, such as family income and maternal level of education, also influenced those outcomes.)

## Sensori-motor Development

Much of the modern research on children's sensori-motor development builds on a theoretical framework constructed by Jean Piaget more than thirty years ago. Piaget established that prior to age two, children are in a "sensori-motor stage" of development. By repeating actions, moving objects, trying them in various combinations, and testing their shapes and compositions, children begin to discover the basic relationships between agents and objects, means and ends. They behave like "little scientists," often showing immense determination to try things in different ways (Piaget, 1951) or repeat the same simple action over and over until it is mastered (Yarrow, 1981; Busch-Rossnagel, 1997).

Piaget's careful observations demonstrated the cognitive basis for egocentrism in young children. They are unable to perceive another point of view (Piaget, 1951). Obviously, sharing and turn-taking are not natural at this age. That does not mean that young children do not feel the beginnings of empathy, as recent research has shown (Zahn-Waxler and Radke-Yarrow, 1982), but the emotional connection seems to come before the cognitive understanding of other points of view.

Piaget's research also explained the phenomenon of stranger anxiety. He demonstrated that very young children simply do not understand that objects are permanent, that they exist even when the child cannot see them. When a 12-month-old child frets as her mother disappears from view, it may be because the child is old enough to recognize her mother as a separate being but not old enough to imagine that her mother still exists when the child cannot see her. A stranger in her place is a reminder that her familiar, beloved mother is not there.

## *The Development of Language and Meaning*

Much that has been learned over the past thirty years about the development of language in children the world over points to the importance of caregivers speaking to children often and in the language they hear at home. Newborn infants are already aware of differences in sounds and voices (Eimas et al., 1971; Brazelton and Cramer, 1990). Caregivers should talk to children from birth onward, long before the children themselves are able to speak. Recent research has found that caregivers throughout the world adopt a "language" called "motherese," a style of slow, distinct, carefully directed, high-pitched speech, when talking to very young children (Fernald et al., 1989). Other research has found that babies are able to decipher where words, even unfamiliar words, start and end in the streams of language they hear (Saffran et al., 1996).

So-called "split screen interaction research" has charted the degree to which infants and their mothers communicate back and forth as they engage each other in cooing and motherese. If the exchange is interrupted, the baby becomes disturbed and saddened, trying to find ways to re-engage the caregiver (Brazelton et al., 1975). Research shows that fathers interact with their babies very differently from mothers. Mothers are more likely to be gentle and soothing, both in voice and manner of holding or moving the baby. Fathers are more likely to play in a rougher, more abrupt fashion, which babies also enjoy (Yogman et al., 1982).

Much recent research on language development has built on the work of another pioneer of early child development, L. S. Vygotsky. Vygotsky and subsequent researchers have shown how adults provide an elaborated account of what the *child* is doing or was recently doing, thereby providing a language scaffold for present or recent actions (Vygotsky, 1934; Nelson, 1996). This kind of *elaboration* later becomes *collaboration* as child and adult together create a narrative about what they are doing or what they did, which helps to cement the actions in the child's understanding and memory. In this way, parents and other adults "mediate" experiences for young children as they (1) focus the child's attention on something (or focus on what already has the child's attention); (2) hold that attention by creating further interest in the object or experience; and (3) connect it to a context that is meaningful to the child (Klein, 1996).

The act of reading to a young child uses skills very similar to the mediation just described. It should be a collaborative activity in which an adult reads *with*—rather than *to*—a child. It is not always necessary to read a book all the way through; the adult can expand both the child's vocabulary and the book's context by encouraging a conversation about what is being "read" as they enjoy the comfort and coziness of doing something together (Whitehurst et al., 1988; Morisset, 1991).

## The Growth of Attachment

The foundation on which all healthy psychological development rests is the development of basic trust—that food will come, that needs will be answered, that warmth and affection will be there, that people can be counted on (Erikson, 1950). Out of this basic trust comes attachment to parents and other primary caregivers. Researchers have made great progress over the past 30 years mapping the growth and development of "attachment" in infants and toddlers. They have found that, by measuring children's reaction to being left alone or with a benign stranger briefly and then reunited with a mother or caregiver, 12-month-old children could be classified as securely or insecurely attached to their mother or other principal caregiver. Any broad sample of toddlers, anywhere throughout the world, will have a substantial majority of children classified as securely attached; a much smaller number will be classified as *anxious/avoidant* or *resistant toward principal caregivers.*

Researchers have found a high correlation between attachment and the caregiver's sensitivity and responsiveness across a variety of cultures (Ainsworth, 1967; Stroufe and Waters, 1977). Children who were classified as securely attached at 12 months were followed over time and showed advanced cognitive, social, and emotional development as they moved into school (Erickson and Pianta, 1989). However, researchers disagree about the answers to three important questions related to attachment (Fox, 1997):

- How much does the child's temperament affect these classifications?
- Is this a truly universal phenomenon for children regardless of culture?
- Are the correlations between early attachment and later performance valid?

Time and future research will establish how later behavior is explained by early attachment.

## Interrelatedness of Areas of Development

For young children, growth in social, emotional, physical, or cognitive areas does not occur in isolation. For example, a crawling baby will look at the expression on her mother's face before attempting something a little bit difficult or scary. If her mother looks pleased, she will proceed; if her mother looks worried, she will stop. This is called "social referencing" (Klinnert et al., 1986). Also, children explore much more vigorously if they feel they have a "safe base," a devoted caregiver to whom to return (Lieberman, 1993). Small babies focus intently on a beloved mother's face for cognitive as well as emotional reasons. The face is probably the child's first experience with an object that changes yet remains the same (Stern, 1985). Games of hiding and finding all have a highly emotional as well as a cognitive content for young children (Lieberman, 1993). And, sadly, a baby who feels no emotional bond may simply stop eating and waste away (Drotar et al., 1994).

## The Sense of "Self"

As very young children grow and become attached to parents and significant adults, they come to "recognize" themselves and develop a sense of "self." Infants and young toddlers are beginning to learn who they are. By seven to nine months they begin to demonstrate expectations of themselves and others (Lewis et al., 1989). By age two they begin to discover their separateness and flex their individual wills (Erikson, 1950; Mahler et al., 1975). However, the "working model" of self is very fragile. It can be so easily affected by how others react to them and treat them that a sharp break in those expectations can compromise the process of individuation itself (Lally, 1995). But, if they are encouraged and sustained by loving and responsive parents and caregivers, children will develop working models of what to expect of themselves and others by the time they are three.

## Individual Differences in Children's Temperament

Research in the first half of the 20th century focused on the commonalities of "normal" development. In the second half of the century, laboratory and clinical research has examined the wide range of normal variations in children's development. Temperament—inborn individual differences in how children react—is one area in which variation is most clearly defined. Thomas and Chess (1977) documented nine variations in temperament:

- Activity level
- Regularity or irregularity of biological rhythms
- Degree of comfort in a new situation

- Adaptability
- Mood
- Intensity of reaction
- Sensitivity threshold
- Distractibility
- Persistence/attention

Researchers are probing the physiological underpinnings for these behavioral differences. For example, individual differences in cortisol levels vary greatly from one child to another as children react to unfamiliar situations, and tend to remain as stable differences over a life span (Kagan et al., 1987). We thus begin to understand that one child might react much more intensely than another to the same situation. What one child perceives as stimulating, another child might perceive as overwhelming. What one child perceives as interesting, another might perceive as frightening. Caregivers need to think about the temperament of each child to be sure they are not demanding too much of an unready child. At the same time, caregivers should not ignore the child who seems flexible and able to amuse himself.

## The Significance of Cultural Diversity

The emerging sense of self begets a cultural or ethnic self, not just a personal self. The cultural self recognizes language, with regional accent and intonation, common food, everyday practices, approaches, values, and ways of responding to others (Phillips, 1988; Chang with Pulido, 1994). Culture has been described as "the invisible curriculum that shapes earliest perceptions of self and society" (Miller, 1989). Obviously, no infant and toddler center can be expected to replicate the child's family situation, but it is important to try to replicate much of what the child is used to at home. This is more easily done when an individual caregiver has the same ethnic, religious, and language background as the child. At the very least, caregivers must be familiar with the diverse traditions of the children's families, respect those diverse traditions, and incorporate some of each culture's traditions into the classroom routines (Far West Laboratory and the California Department of Education, 1995).

## Conclusion

This chapter has sketched, very briefly, some highlights from research on infant and toddler development over the past thirty years. It serves as a background for the chapters that follow. For those who wish to learn more about the research, extensive references are listed at the end of this book.

# CHAPTER 3

# INFANTS AND TODDLERS IN THEIR FAMILIES AND COMMUNITIES

# 3. INFANTS AND TODDLERS
# IN THEIR FAMILIES AND COMMUNITIES

It does not require research scientists to tell us what has been understood for centuries: the family is the most important influence in the life of young children, and each family needs help and support in raising their children. Infant and toddler centers are part of that support. This chapter reviews recent research indicating that factors which directly affect parents often have an indirect effect on the subsequent development of their infants and toddlers. This research results from studies conducted in the fields of sociology and epidemiology as well as developmental psychology.

## Risk Factors and Protective Factors

Most children are born with internal strengths that, combined with environmental "helping hands," enable them to construct the "armor" needed to withstand the stresses of life. For example, a pleasantly flexible child who is born into a family with manageable stresses, and who has an adoring family and responsive caregivers, accumulates a set of protective factors that will serve him well. Conversely, if a child is born prematurely, if he is highly sensitive to noise or colors or touch, if he is in a noisy and chaotic environment, and if his parents—who have no experience or advice in how to cope—decide to leave him alone to avoid upsetting him, the child will accumulate a set of risk factors that put him at a disadvantage now and in the future (Greenspan & Weider, 1993; Rutter, 1979; Sameroff et al., 1987; Beckwith, 1990).

## How the Newborn Infant Affects Family and Community

The arrival of a new baby is an exciting event that brings offers of help from extended family and neighbors. We know how important family and neighborhood resources, including relatives, neighbors, friends, churches, peer groups, social clubs, sports clubs, and fellow workers can be to the well-being of a family with an infant (Dunst and Trivette, 1990; Weissbourd, 1996).

And yet, however adorable, new babies put families under stress. Routines are interrupted, fathers and siblings take second place, and no one sleeps enough or without interruption. A mother may feel incompetent, and her mother or mother-in-law may give her more advice than she is ready to hear. She may even become temporarily depressed. Fortunately, fathers can play a key role in supporting strong maternal-infant attachment and helping to reduce stress on the mother (Belsky and Isabella, 1988; Pruett, 1987).

## How Children and Families Influence Each Other

Over the years, it has been common to think of adults and their environment as affecting the development of the infant or toddler, but it is also necessary to look at the wealth of recent research on the effect of the baby on the family. Researchers have found a significant reciprocal effect between child and family. For example, the child who receives warm, sensitive care generally develops a positive set of behaviors which, in turn, evoke more warm, sensitive responses from her care-givers, encouraging the child, and so on. (Stern, 1985). In fact, an unusually responsive child can elicit surprising amounts of interest and support from adults simply because her responsiveness appeals to and rewards the adults (Werner, 1982). In contrast, an unusually fussy baby or aggressive toddler may provoke negative reactions in caregivers which, in turn, bring forth even more fussy or aggressive behavior by the child (Sameroff and Fiesse, 1990). It is important for the adults in the child's life to be aware of these patterns and be sensitive to the child's nonverbal messages.

## How Family Income Levels Affect Children's Development

Families who can afford to feed their children nutritious, well-balanced diets, provide toys and books, play with and read to their children, and are able to manage daily stresses, are in a position favorable to their children's development. When family income is inadequate to provide those supports, children's healthy development is less certain (Duncan et al., 1994; Halpern, 1993). One particularly dramatic piece of research demonstrates the effects of poverty across generations. Researchers studied a large sample of American children whose family income had dropped to one-third of its previous level during the Great Depression of the 1930s, and compared them with children in families whose income remained stable. Children who were in their teens at the time of the study seemed to have been unaffected. On the other hand, children under age six were profoundly affected by the drop in family income. Furthermore, these affected children's offspring had poorer outcomes than the offspring of their peers with stable family income (Elder, 1974).

## *How Child Care Programs Affect Children's Development*

Thus far we have looked at factors which are known to affect the families of infants and toddlers. Infant and toddler child care certainly supports families, and influences the development of the children themselves.

Recent research on the effects of group care on infants and toddlers in the United States has found that *quality* child care programs for this age group are very beneficial to children (Hayes et al., 1990). "Quality" is defined by one set of researchers as "stable child care arrangements featuring skilled, sensitive, and motivated caregivers" (NCCIP, 1988). Quality child care does *not* interfere with the security of infants' attachments to parents (USDHHS/NICHD, 1996). On the contrary, it has long term cognitive, social, and emotional benefits, particularly for children from poor families (Ramey et al., 1985; Lally et al., 1988; Caughy et al., 1994).

The key word is *quality*. Several studies have directly related the quality of the programs — as defined by factors such as group size, child/staff ratios, and caregivers' training— with higher scores of children on standardized cognitive measures (Ruopp et al., 1979; National Child Care Staffing Study, 1989; Cost, Quality, and Child Outcomes Study Team, 1995). Another study of children in the state of Florida showed impressive changes in the children's cognitive competence after improvements were made in program quality (Howes et al., 1995). The kind of care offered makes a difference to the children, both directly to the children themselves and indirectly through the support it gives their families in their parenting role. Quality child care is worth the financial investment.

## *Other Factors That Affect Children's Development*

Two other factors are of major importance to families who are raising infants and toddlers. The first is job-related stress; the second is community violence. Both factors affect children because both directly affect their parents' stress levels (Galinsky et al., 1993; Osofsky, 1997).

## *Conclusion*

There is a complex relationship between the child, his family, his community, and his experiences in a child care center. When the relationship is strong, children benefit. However, it is of the utmost importance that infant and toddler programs be of high quality—the kind of program outlined and described in the chapters that follow.

# PART III

# HOW INFANTS AND TODDLERS LEARN

3

# HOW INFANTS AND TODDLERS LEARN

Infants and toddlers are learning all the time. Emotionally, they are learning from their earliest days that the world surrounding them is a caring, responsive, and interesting place, or an unloving, neglectful, and frightening one. Furthermore, they are beginning to tailor their actions to fit those perceptions of that world, what it expects from them, and what they expect of it. That context is the emotional foundation in which all other learning occurs.

In cognitive and physical terms, infants and toddlers are highly efficient little "learning machines," designed to absorb and classify information and knowledge. As described in Chapter 2, their brain cells are undergoing an amazing process of wiring, simultaneously organizing and pruning the trillions of connections being made. Even the infant brain has the capacity to generalize, or categorize. For example, an infant can classify sounds as "the same" or "new." A toddler knows that a particular chair she has never seen before belongs in the "chair" category. She can sort objects by color, size, or shape long before she can label these categories. Somehow a young child learns to connect the singular experience to other like experiences. Even more amazing, a young child can understand complex language structure, such as, when *you* are speaking, "you" means me and "I" means you, but when *I* am speaking, "you" means you and "I" means me.

Infants' and toddlers' capacity for learning is truly extraordinary, but can be limited by certain conditions. In order to exercise their phenomenal ability to learn, young children must:

- Be *ready to learn* (not sleepy, tired, hungry, sick, or anxious)
- Be *interested* and *focused* on the activity at hand
- Have *chosen* to engage in that activity

Young children learn best by doing. They need to play with the object they are focused on—exploring it by pushing, pulling, twisting, tasting, stacking, turning it upside down, etc. Because infants and toddlers learn by exploring, the best way to encourage learning is to follow their lead, talk about what they are doing, and help them expand their exploration. At the same time, caregivers also need to expose infants and toddlers to a full variety of experiences that will help them learn. When parents ask, "What will you teach my child?", teachers can tell them about the variety of activities and experiences that make up a balanced curriculum. Chapters 4 through 9 set forth the recommended practices, activities, toys, and materials that together comprise a well-rounded curriculum for infants and toddlers. In a child-centered methodology, activities emanate from the interests, needs, and developmental level of each child. It is premised on the belief that no particular experience or activity should ever be forced on a child.

Group activity does not work well for young children, especially when the activity is chosen by the teacher. How, then, can she be sure each child is exposed to the full variety of experiences? A caregiver may decide that children will learn about shapes this week. She simply makes toys with triangles, squares, and rectangles available to the children to pick up and work with, at their own pace. When they do, she watches them, praises them, and may make suggestions to further the child's exploration. In other words, she does not require that each child complete particular exercises involving shapes. The caregiver is a facilitator, not a commander. She lets the child's interests guide him as he explores the infant- and toddler-centered curriculum.

Chapter 4 discusses emotional milestones. Chapters 5 through 8 outline the elements of a child-centered curriculum that promotes social development, cognitive development, language development, and physical development. Chapter 9 shows the many ways in which even daily routines can be an opportunity for learning in an emotionally supportive context. Chapter 10 offers suggestions for how caregivers can incorporate systematic observation of infants and toddlers into their program. Finally, Chapter 11 describes how caregivers and families can work together to support infants' and toddlers' development and learning.

# CHAPTER 4

# SUPPORTING EMOTIONAL DEVELOPMENT

# 4. SUPPORTING EMOTIONAL DEVELOPMENT

Clearly, the ways caregivers respond to children can either enhance or inhibit their emotional development. A child's emotional development is as important as his physical, cognitive, social, and language development and calls for the same level of sensitivity and support on the part of parents and caregivers. This chapter discusses the role of emotions in children's lives, children's emotional development, adult qualities and behaviors that support children's emotional development, adult behaviors that harm children's emotional development, how to talk to children about their emotions, and how to help children express their emotions.

## The Role of Emotions in Children's Lives

Young children develop many emotions throughout infancy and toddlerhood. They experience joy and affection, anger and frustration, sadness and shame, fear and anxiety, trust and contentment, and pride. As the following examples illustrate, caregivers are likely to be exposed to a broad range of children's emotions in a single day.

> *"Peek-a-boo" says the teacher, showing her face from behind her hands. Baby Vera laughs with joy.*

> *Two toddlers struggle over a wooden toy each wants for herself. Their faces are red with anger.*

> *Jamie cries when his cookie breaks into his milk. He wanted it to stay whole.*

> *Eighteen-month-old Matthew hides behind his mother while she talks to the teacher.*

There are no right or wrong feelings, and all emotions play an essential role in children's lives. Most important, emotions provide children—and their caregivers—with information about their well-being. Positive feelings, like happiness and trust, give children a sense of safety and security. These emotions tell children that all is right with the world and prompt them to repeat pleasurable experiences. Other emotions feel bad and signal danger or discontent. They alert children to the fact that something is wrong. Anger causes children to confront obstacles. Sadness brings a drop in energy, allowing children time and quiet to adjust to loss or disappointment. Fear leads children to protect themselves. Affection signals to children that they are lovable, valuable, and competent.

Because all emotions have lessons to teach, adults must work together to help children understand their emotions, become more sensitive to the feelings of others, and find effective ways to cope with the many emotions they experience.

This process begins at birth and continues throughout the preschool years. The most important step caregivers and parents can take to support children's emotional development is to model healthy emotional expression with consistency, comfort, and encouragement throughout their child's development.

## *Children's Emotional Development*

Emotional development in infancy and toddlerhood is marked by progressive change. When two-week-old Nancy is startled by a loud noise, she recoils, not out of true fear, but simply as a reflexive reaction to an unexpected event. She has not yet developed the thought processes necessary to interpret what she is experiencing emotionally. However, children experience real joy (at about six weeks), anger (at approximately four months), sadness (at approximately five to seven months) and fear (at approximately six to nine months). These early core emotions are very intense, which explains why infants and toddlers exhibit such dramatic emotional outbursts. By the end of the third year, children's emotions have become increasingly *differentiated*—for example, joy, an original core emotion, becomes differentiated to contentment, excitement, or pleasure.

Another characteristic of infants' and toddlers' emotional development is that their emotional responses alternate rapidly. One minute a child may scream, "No!" and the next minute crawl into your lap for a hug. The quick change from one emotional state to another is universally recognized as typical for children this age.

From infancy through their third birthday, children work through two significant emotional stages: developing trust and autonomy. Each stage is characterized by positive and negative extremes and a central emotional task of resolving the conflict that arises between the two extremes. Although all children experience both the positive and negative aspects of each stage, healthy emotional development occurs when their experiences are weighted in favor of the positive. These stages build on one another, with the first serving as the foundation for the next.

## Developing Trust

During their first months of life, infants either develop basic feelings of security and trust, or they develop a sense of hopelessness and uncertainty that leads to mistrust. If babies do not develop trusting feelings at this time, it is more difficult to acquire them later. Along with parents, caregivers play a key role in providing the kinds of relationships and experiences that enable infants to develop confidence in themselves, in the world, and in the people around them.

> *Feelings of security and trust develop out of relations with others. Infants cannot develop these on their own. They develop these feelings from the way other people treat them. . . Two adult behaviors of special importance are responding immediately to infant distress signals and responding constantly to children's signals of distress, need or pleasure.*
>
> (Wilson et al., 1995, p. 212)

Children who develop positive feelings of trust at this stage learn, "I am lovable and my world is safe and secure."

## Developing Autonomy

Sometime during their second year, toddlers who have developed a strong sense of trust begin to move toward greater independence. The fundamental issue throughout this stage is whether the child emerges as a self-directed human being or one with basic misgivings about self-worth. Autonomous children do what they can for themselves. They also know they can take advantage of help and guidance from others while still maintaining some ideas of their own. Overly dependent children doubt their ability to control their world or themselves and rely on others to make decisions and do things for them.

It is normal for children of this age to shift back and forth from an autonomous to a dependent mode in a short time. One moment they want to explore; the next, they want to be in your lap.

## *Adult Qualities and Behaviors That Support Children's Emotional Development*

Children's emotional development is enhanced when they view the adults in their lives as sources of comfort and encouragement. Caregivers communicate emotional support and promote self-confidence through *genuine* displays of warmth, responsiveness, respect, empathy, and acceptance toward each child in their care.

## Promoting Self-Confidence

Children who develop a healthy sense of autonomy and self-confidence are those who are given numerous opportunities for exploration and mastery. In contrast, children develop a dominant sense of shame and doubt when opportunities to explore are withheld, when their attempts at independence are met with impatience or disapproval, and when they are not permitted to make any decisions for themselves. Parents and caregivers use several strategies to promote autonomy among young children:

- Give children choices. Let them decide which cup to use, which story to read, which fruit to eat, which activity to try, or which hand to wash first.
- Encourage children to do things for themselves. They can pour their own juice, dress themselves as much as possible, and help clean up after play.
- Create safe opportunities for children to experiment with materials without prescribing a "correct way." Let them try paints at the easel, blocks, or materials at the water table.
- Encourage children to physically explore the environment. They can climb a hill, balance on a low beam, or jump from a safe step.
- Repeat activities so children have many chances to practice and improve their skills.
- Give children ample time to work with each material so they can experiment, make choices, and experience the results of their actions.

Toddlers who achieve a sense of autonomy learn, "I can make decisions; I can do things on my own."

## Genuineness

Genuineness means adults are truthful, but also reasonable and encouraging. To demonstrate genuineness:

- Be clear about something that is not working; avoid giving false hope.
- Stay nearby to encourage children as they attempt things on their own.
- Thank children for helping or trying.
- Explain your reasons for doing something that a child may not, at first, want to do.

## Warmth

Warmth involves showing interest in children, being friendly toward them, and responding to them. Adults who demonstrate warmth help children feel comfortable, supported, and valued. To show warmth and caring:

- Be physically available to children.
- Touch children gently.
- Make frequent eye contact.
- Talk to children at every opportunity.
- Get down to toddlers' eye level when talking to them.

## Responsiveness

When adults respond in loving and predictable ways, children expect to be safe and comfortable most of the time, and their view of the world is hopeful. The caregiver's consistent responsiveness to the child and the type of relationship that develops between them are important factors in determining the degree to which young children thrive. Consistency of care is enhanced when caregivers are assigned to certain children and interact with them throughout the day. Through the relationship that develops from daily contact between teacher and child, the child's world becomes more safe and predictable. To demonstrate responsiveness, caregivers:

- Respond promptly to an infant's cries by picking up the child and attending to her needs.
- Confer with parents and other family members about each child's routine. (For example, what soothing strategies work best with the child?)
- Establish regular patterns of care that answer to each child's cues. (For example, Tanya likes to be rocked right before taking her nap, but Jen prefers a gentle back rub).
- Caress infants whenever opportunities arise.

## Respect

Having respect for children means believing they are capable human beings who have the capacity to learn. To demonstrate respect:

- Get to know children as individuals.
- Encourage children to work toward their own solutions.
- Invite children to communicate their ideas.

## Empathy

The ability to recognize and understand another person's point of view is the definition of empathy. An empathic caregiver responds to the child's affective or emotional state by experiencing some of the same emotion. Teachers can convey and demonstrate empathy toward children in a number of ways:

- "Tune in" to children's moods.
- Mirror children's feelings with your face and voice.
- Echo infants' sounds.
- Label children's emotions using simple, non-judgmental statements. ("You look happy.")
- Encourage the natural beginnings of empathy towards other children. ("That was a nice hug.")
- Use words to respond to toddlers' gestures. ("You want a peach.")
- Repeat and expand toddlers' statements. (Child: "Shoe." Teacher: "You like your red shoes.")

## Acceptance

Acceptance means being valued unconditionally regardless of physical appearance, family background, abilities, or behavior. Without acceptance, healthy emotional development is impossible. Children interpret the following adult behaviors as signs of acceptance:

- Use children's names when talking to them, but do not use names as substitutes for the words "no" or "stop."
- Interact with each child frequently during the day in a friendly, interested way.
- Identify something likeable about each child as you interact with him.
- Pay close attention to children when they are talking.
- Acknowledge children's attempts to do things. Do not insist on "perfection."

A child may express an unexpected emotion such as fear when other children laugh at a dog in a story. The caregivers should be watchful to understand the reason behind the emotion.

## *Harmful Adult Behaviors*

Children learn how to manage their emotions through interactions with others. They watch how people deal with emotions and gain information from how they are treated in emotional situations. Depending on the nature of these interactions children learn either helpful lessons or harmful ones about emotions and their expression.

Caregivers must examine the words they use and their motivations so that they do not unwittingly inhibit the development of healthy emotional skills in the children they care for. Adult behaviors can be harmful.

Adults often resort to harmful behaviors—forcing, denying, misrepresenting reality, and allowing sudden shifts in behavior—when they are trying to avoid a scene or want to minimize the intensity of the moment. Such strategies have the opposite effect. They not only make matters worse, but they also prevent children from learning more effective ways to handle emotional situations. In place of these destructive practices, adults can use alternative strategies to promote children's feelings of trust, competence, and worth, and help them increase their interpersonal skills.

| Helpful Emotional Lessons | Harmful Emotional Lessons |
|---|---|
| 1. Emotions are a natural part of every day life. | 1. Some emotions are good; others are bad. |
| 2. It is okay to let people know how you feel. | 2. It is not okay to let people know how you feel. |
| 3. There are a variety of constructive ways to express all kinds of emotions. | 3. There are few effective ways to express emotions. |

## *Helpful Adult Behaviors*

To avoid adult behaviors that thwart emotional development, caregivers should use the preferred behaviors described below.

### Acknowledge children's fears; do not force children when they are fearful.

In the mistaken belief that children will overcome a fear by facing it directly, some adults force children to confront what they fear most. Rarely does this relieve the child's fear. Instead, the fear is often intensified and, in some cases, may last a lifetime. When adults ignore children's emotional signals, children learn that their feelings are unimportant or wrong. Coercing children also betrays their sense of trust. Acknowledge children's fears and allow them to overcome those fears gradually.

### Acknowledge children's emotions; do not deny them.

Sometimes adults deny children's feelings by actually forbidding certain emotions. Directives like "Don't be afraid," or "You shouldn't be angry," or "Let's see you smile, no more tears," deny children's emotions. At other times, adults may dismiss the importance of children's emotions with remarks like "That's nothing to be scared about," or "You know it won't be so bad." Adults who say such things are often well-intentioned but, unfortunately, statements like these tell children that their emotions are wrong and they are bad for experiencing them. A more supportive strategy is to acknowledge children's feelings as they occur, and then explain why it is necessary to do something another way.

Making fun of children or embarrassing them out of their emotions is a destructive practice. Adults hurt children when they say things like "Don't be such a baby," or "You don't want me to tell your grandma you were being bad, do you?" Shaming makes children feel mistrustful, doubtful, and inadequate. It certainly does not cause them to respond more positively or make them feel better. The best way to keep from accidentally embarrassing young children is to remind yourself that their emotions are very real and legitimate to them.

### Acknowledge painful situations; do not misrepresent reality.

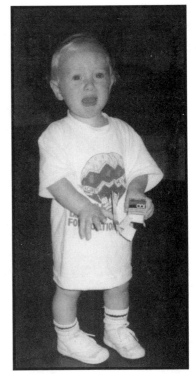

Sometimes, in an effort to protect children from difficult emotional experiences, adults misrepresent what will happen. For instance, Boris is afraid of having his finger poked for a blood test, and the nurse attempts to soothe him by saying "This won't hurt a bit." But it really does hurt a little. It is better to say "It will hurt a little and then it will be over." Likewise, Elizabeth is upset that her mother is preparing to leave the building. The teacher says, "She's not really leaving, she's just going down to the office." Such misconceptions fail to prepare children for the reality of the situations they are facing and damage their trust in the adult. An emotionally attuned caregiver would say, "I know you are sad to see mama leave, but she will come back to get you." Giving children accurate information in simple language is the best way to avoid this pitfall.

## Practice consistent behavior; do not allow sudden shifts in behavior.

Children often are not surprised by the actions of adults, since so much that adults do is hard to understand. However, adults who suddenly change from cheerful to angry or from attentive to neglectful for no apparent reason instill fear and wariness in children. It is important to explain to children what is going to happen next and then to behave in a trustworthy, predictable manner.

## *Talking to Children About Their Emotions*

Parents naturally start talking to children about emotions almost from birth. In group care, it is important to continue acquainting children with an "emotion vocabulary." Because children learn most comprehensively within the context of personal experience, they benefit when their emotions are named and described to them as they occur. For instance, when Katherine is angry and her caregiver says, "Katherine, you look angry," the caregiver is directly relating the experience to the concept of anger. The adult shows a child that her emotional state is describable and illustrates that talking about emotions is a good way to begin dealing with them. As caregivers practice the techniques below, children become more understanding about their own emotions and those of others.

## Observe children carefully.

The context of a situation is important to its meaning. Pay close attention to children's facial expressions, voice tone, and body movements, as well as any sounds or words they might say. Some feelings are extreme, some are more moderate, some are positive, and some are negative, but all emotions are important to talk about.

## Name the child's emotion.

Identify what the child is feeling in a short statement to the child. Keep your words simple: "You seem upset," or "You look pleased."

## Use a variety of "feeling words."

Use many different words to describe the whole range of emotions children experience. Begin by using words to describe the core emotions: happy, angry, sad, and afraid. Gradually, use related words like pleased, disappointed, annoyed, or thrilled. Use your body, face, and voice to make the meaning of unfamiliar words more clear. Add another sentence to define the word you have used: "Joseph, you look frustrated. You can't get that puzzle to work." Although very young children will not understand every word, naming children's emotions will get you into the habit of observing children more closely. As children mature, your statements will have more meaning and will help them better understand what they are feeling.

## Help children recognize other people's feelings.

Learning to get along with others requires children to recognize how other people are feeling in various situations. This skill emerges slowly with maturity and practice.

- Describe how other people are feeling. Point out the specific behavior cues that tell how another is feeling and put that feeling into words: "Lara is laughing. She is happy," or "Stephen is crying. That means he is unhappy."
- Draw children's attention to events that trigger people's emotions. "Sophie's mother is coming to read us a story today. Sophie is very happy about that."

## *Helping Children Express Their Emotions to Others*

Young children mistakenly believe that others automatically know how they feel in certain situations, but they need adult support and encouragement to express their feelings in words. Caregivers and parents can set examples, help children put their feelings into words, acknowledge children's strong emotions, and avoid destructive behaviors.

## Talk about feelings.

Include emotions in your casual conversations by telling how everyday events affect you: "I'm happy to see the sun is out," or "I wish it would stop raining." Discuss events in terms of people's feelings: "We have new playdough today. I know that will make Sarah happy." Ask children how they feel about everyday occurrences: "We have apples for snack. Who here likes apples?"

## Help children put their feelings into words.

Begin by asking children simple yes or no questions that focus on their feelings: "Sarah took your paint brush. Billy, did you like it when she did that?" Use Billy's answer to prompt Sarah to become more aware of his feelings. As children gain practice, give them simple words to express themselves. "You didn't like it when Sarah took your brush. Say, 'I don't like that.'" Then use more open-ended inquiries: "Sarah took your paint brush. Tell her how that makes you feel." In time, children learn to use these sample "scripts" without adult prompting.

## Acknowledge children's emotions and prevent destructive behaviors.

First label the child's emotion: "You are very angry." Follow this acknowledgment with a statement like "It's all right to be angry, but I can't let you hit. Hitting hurts." Gently guide the child to a more constructive solution.

## *Conclusion*

This chapter describes how very young children's emotions develop and change over time, and how they slowly become aware of their feelings and those of others. It is important for the adult caregivers to be aware of this development, and be supportive and nurturing throughout the process. The next chapter, *Guiding Social Development*, describes how emotions develop as children become part of a group.

# CHAPTER 5

# GUIDING SOCIAL DEVELOPMENT

# 5. GUIDING SOCIAL DEVELOPMENT

Children are social beings. From the moment they are born, they begin a lifetime of interdependence and active involvement with other people. Through social interactions, children learn about themselves, gain knowledge of human relationships, and develop interpersonal skills. As children mature socially, they also come to understand the rules and values of the society in which they live. Infants and toddlers do not inherently know these things. Such understanding evolves slowly and may be enhanced or inhibited by the social environment.

Social relations change as children age and develop. This chapter examines the role of caregivers in supporting early social relationships and socialization, and presents strategies for responding to difficult and challenging behaviors.

## Social Relations in Infancy and Toddlerhood

**Young infants** (birth to 8 months) are born with a capacity and need for social contact. Their needs are best met through stimulating, consistent, caring interactions with a few familiar adults who get to know them as individuals.

**Mobile infants** (9 to 17 months) are curious about others but need assistance and supervision in interacting with peers. They continue to need one or a few familiar adults as their primary social partners.

**Toddlers** (18 to 36 months) are eager to make contact with other children. However, they need continued adult support and guidance to initiate interactions, maintain relationships with peers, and negotiate the conflicts that arise naturally among beginners in the social arena. Toddlers continue to rely on familiar adults to provide a "safe base" from which to explore the social environment.

## The Role of Caregivers

Because caregivers and teachers are among the first people with whom children develop relationships, they play an important role in supporting infants' and toddlers' social development:

- **First and foremost, caregivers and parents convey to children a sense of love and acceptance.** This security helps children feel good about themselves and provides a foundation from which children develop affection and respect for others.

- **Second, caregivers help children develop the social skills they will need to maintain satisfying relationships with adults and peers.** Learning to get along, share, take turns, cooperate, and make friends are major social tasks of early childhood.

- **Finally, caregivers help children learn right from wrong.** This process is termed socialization, meaning that children are gradually socialized to adopt behaviors valued by the community.

## Supporting Children's Early Social Relationships

Caregivers use many techniques to promote positive social relationships between children and adults and among children and their peers.

- **They ensure that each child has a special relationship with one particular teacher.** Consistent social and emotional support is particularly critical during the first three years of life. Through close, continuous relationships with their caregivers, children learn to trust other people and feel good about themselves.

- **They create opportunities for infants and toddlers to interact with one another throughout the day.** Make sure children have opportunities to interact with a few children at a time as well as larger numbers in the group. Toddlers can easily become overwhelmed by too many people at once.

- **They create spaces where children can observe if they choose.** Not every child wants to join activities with other children. Some children like to watch before joining an activity. Others like to take a "break" from vigorous play. A platform or window seat are ideal spaces from which children can observe the action of the room.

- **They provide enough space and materials for children to use while playing together.** Mobile infants and toddlers are unable to stop quickly and often have poor balance in the early stages of walking. They need enough uncluttered space to avoid getting in each other's way. Duplicate play materials minimize arguments over toys, since sharing is not easy for children this age. Make sure there are enough similar toys so young children can play together without conflict. "Sebastian, here is some blue playdough for you. Hilda, there is some blue for you, too."

- **They help children learn and use each other's names.** Use children's names often as you interact with them. Say the names of the children with whom they are playing or who are close by.

- **They help children develop an awareness of their peers.** Draw children's attention to one another by making comments like, "Sonya, you are using the red paint. George, you are using red paint too." Or, "Golda likes the *Billy Goats Gruff* story. Helga likes *The Funny Fisherman*."

- **They encourage and praise children in the early expressions of caring and sympathy for others.** If Sonya gives George a toy because he is crying, praise her.

- **They help children recognize friendly overtures from peers.** The caregiver must constantly verbalize social situations. When Alexa puts her arm on Michael's back and leans on him, say, "Michael, Alexa is giving you a hug." When a child pushes a toy car toward another child, say, "Anna is showing you her car."

## Socialization

Socialization is the process of learning the rules and mores of one's society. For infants and toddlers it distinguishes appropriate from unacceptable behaviors. They learn these distinctions through interactions with the significant adults in their lives.

**Young infants** (birth to 8 months) begin to adapt their eating and sleeping habits in accordance with their own increasingly regularized internal rhythms and the social expectations conveyed through the gentle guidance of sensitive caregivers. Infants require no overt disciplinary action. Their primary task is to establish trust in adults and the world. The extent to which this is accomplished directly affects children's responsiveness to adult guidance later in life.

**Mobile infants** (9 to 17 months) are eager to act on the world but have little understanding of what is permissible and what is not. They cannot remember rules or think through situations. Instead, they experiment with a variety of behaviors to meet their needs and satisfy their desires. The adult role at this time is to provide consistent limits on children's behavior within a warm, loving relationship.

**Toddlers** (18 to 36 months) are just beginning to develop a sense of ownership. They also have difficulty recognizing that others may have intentions that conflict with their own. They are not ready to share and are unable to accommodate others' needs. The result is a continual testing of social boundaries. Such testing is normal and requires patient, supportive guidance from teachers and family members as children are helped toward increasing flexibility and cooperation in social settings.

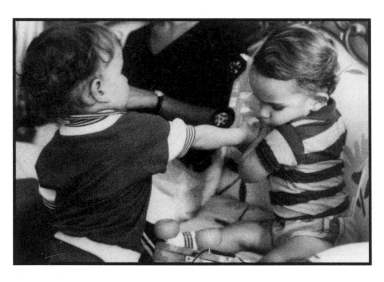

## Strategies That Support Early Childhood Socialization

Throughout the early years, socialization is an ongoing experimental process. When children violate social norms they do so out of lack of experience and skill, not as a result of character flaws or simply to annoy grown-ups. Adults use strategies of modeling, substitution and redirection, rules, and appropriate consequences to guide children's behavior in positive ways.

## Modeling

Children discover how to behave by watching others. Setting a good example teaches children right from wrong. They learn powerful lessons when they observe their teachers treating others with kindness, telling the truth, using reasoning to solve problems, or offering help to someone in need. It is also important to model politeness. Even though infants cannot be expected to say "please" and "thank you," it is never too early for children to understand that courtesy and good manners are a regular part of appropriate behavior.

Modeling is most effective when the positive behavior is pointed out to children. By combining actions with words, children recognize appropriate behaviors they might not otherwise notice. For instance, if the caregiver wipes the table after snack, the child will not recognize the helpful behavior unless she says, "I am wiping the table so it will be clean. Here is a sponge for you. You can help too."

## Substitution and Redirection

Substitution and redirection involve getting the child's attention, then offering an alternative object that might be of interest. Both strategies distract children from less appropriate actions or objectives. Harsh verbal demands, or simply pulling an object out of a child's hands with no replacement, are less effective techniques and lead to angry confrontations that are unnecessary.

For example, Fanny, age 18 months, is exploring objects in the block area when she discovers a pair of eye glasses someone mistakenly left on a low shelf. Noticing this, the teacher offers her a wooden giraffe. The child lets go of the glasses in order to grasp the toy animal. The teacher puts the spectacles up and out of sight and then spends the next few minutes playing with Fanny, stacking blocks, and making fences around the giraffe. Fanny shifts her attention from the glasses to the blocks and giraffe, participating happily as a result of the teacher's substitution.

Later in the day, 28-month-old Sammy discovers the loud noise he can make when he flushes the toilet. He is found in the bathroom several times, happily flushing the toilet over and over again. The teacher lets him know he can flush one more time and then she escorts him back into the room. Once there, she and Sammy select a story to read. The teacher seats Sammy on her lap and begins the tale. In this way she physically redirects him away from the bathroom and into a more acceptable activity.

## Rules

Rules, like invisible fences that provide boundaries, are guides for behavior. Gradually, as two-year-olds begin to learn rules, they recognize what they can and cannot do. Such recognition gives children a sense of security and confidence, but takes a long time to achieve. In the meantime, children frequently test rules to make sure they will hold. Some children do more testing than others, but all children need to learn there are limits to what is allowed (Gonzalez-Mena and Eyer, 1997). How well children learn these lessons has much to do with how adults make rules and enforce them. Rules should be specific, stated in positive terms, and have clear reasons for being followed.

- **Effective rules are specific.** Both the teacher and the child understand exactly what is expected. It is more likely that a child will take only one cracker at snack time if the teacher says, "Just take one cracker," then if she says, "Don't take too many crackers." The teacher's idea of too many may be more than one, but the child's idea may be quite different.

- **Effective rules are stated in positive terms.** They tell children what to do versus what not to do or what to stop doing. It is easier for children to learn how to substitute words for actions when teachers say, "Tell her 'my turn,'" instead of "Don't hit!" Children will more likely remember to wear mittens when the rule is, "Wear your mittens!" than when they are told "Don't forget your mittens." The following table shows how to turn negative statements into positive rules.

| <u>Negative Statement</u> | <u>Positive Rule</u> |
|---|---|
| Don't gulp your food. | Let's eat slowly. |
| Don't choke the guinea pig. | Hold the guinea pig gently, like this. |
| Don't yell. | Let's talk softly. |
| Don't kick. | Please keep your feet still. |
| Don't grab. | Sonja wants a turn. |
| Don't color on the wall. | Color on the paper, please. |

Telling children how to behave and showing them desirable actions gives children the direction they need to be successful.

- **Effective rules include reasons.** Reasons help rules make sense and give children specific information about why adults approve or disapprove of certain behaviors. By the time children are eight- to ten-months old, they can begin to comprehend simple reasons behind basic rules if those reasons are explained in relevant situations. At this age, it makes sense to a toddler when you put cookies in the oven and say, "Stay away from the oven. It is hot. If you touch it you could get burned." Remember, however, that *comprehension should not be confused with learning and retention.* Infants and toddlers need constant supervision and many reminders.

Children do not develop the internal controls necessary to actually follow rules on their own until the later preschool or even elementary years. Teachers may wonder whether there is any value in reasoning with very young children, since it takes so long for them to learn basic rules. *The evidence suggests that giving children reasons is the single most important factor in the later development of self-directed behavior.* Thus, the reasons behind the rules play an important role in the socialization process. Teachers use reasons most effectively when they follow these guidelines:

√ **Give reasons every time you set a rule**. Do not assume children will remember the reason simply because you know it or because you have stated it many times before. Children often forget or do not realize that a current situation is similar to one they have encountered in the past.

√ **Keep reasons simple**. Focus on health and safety, protecting peoples' rights, and protecting property. For instance, "Stay with me so I'll know you are safe." Or, "Wait. Joseph isn't finished using the red crayon." Or, "Turn the pages gently so the book won't tear."

√ **Explain.** "Walk, so you won't fall," is more effective than "Walk, because that's the rule at our school." "Put the toys in the box so we can find them later," makes more sense to children than, "Put the toys in the box because I said so!"

## Appropriate Consequences

Consequences are the results of behavior and determine whether a particular behavior is likely to happen in the future. Positive consequences encourage repeated behaviors; corrective consequences reduce them. All consequences must be appropriate to the ages and needs of the children in your care.

**Positive Consequences** A smile, a hug, a pat on the back, words of encouragement and praise are all ways to let children know you approve of something they have done.

Try to notice children attempting to follow the rule, and let them know you appreciate their efforts, even if they are not totally successful. These positive interactions encourage children to keep trying and help them remember positive behaviors another time.

**Corrective Consequences**   The most effective corrective consequences are ones directly related to the rule. There is an obvious connection, a "logical consequence," between the child's behavior and the guidance the adult provides. The use of logical consequences helps children understand the direct results of the rule. For instance, if Rudolph is throwing toys on the floor, a logical consequence is to have him help put the toys back. When Sally throws sand in another child's eyes, a logical consequence is for her to assist the teacher in washing the sand out. In both cases, such consequences show children that inappropriate behaviors are not allowed and help correct the negative behaviors. Banishing the children from the room or having them sit in a chair for five minutes does not provide the same beneficial lessons.

## *The Basics of Child Guidance*

- **Use short, simple statements to make your expectations known.** Too many words confuse young children.

- **Select only a few rules** at any one time. Too many rules are difficult to enforce and promote feelings of shame and doubt in young children.

- **Be consistent** in your enforcement of rules. It is difficult for children to figure out what is expected if the rules change from day to day or from child to child. For instance, if the rule is, "Wash your hands after toileting," this rule must be enforced each time toileting occurs. Consistent enforcement makes rules more predictable and easier to follow.

- **State rules as suggestions, not mandates.** Toddlers respond especially well to positive rules that are stated as suggestions. For instance, "Let's hang up our coats," instead of "You must hang up your coat now."

- **Use "please" and "thank you."** Courtesy sets a tone of cooperation and models the way people are expected to behave.

- **Focus on children's behavior, and don't make judgments about a child's character.** Say, "It makes me sad when you hit. Hitting hurts." Or, "Thank you for throwing away your napkin." Avoid saying things like, "I don't like little boys who hit," or, "You're such a good girl for throwing away your napkin."

- **Talk and act simultaneously.** Immediately stop children's actions that may be harmful to themselves or others. For instance, if two toddlers are struggling over a toy, stop the hitting by grasping their hands or separating the toddlers. If a child is about to jump off a high platform move quickly to restrain her. Once the dangerous situation is past, children are better able to hear what you have to say.

- **Implement rules and consequences patiently.** Young children are newcomers to society. They cannot be expected to comply with rules on demand. Treat children as novices who are learning. If children have difficulty following a rule, try to:

  √ Repeat your words more slowly and clearly.
  √ Rephrase your message in simpler terms.
  √ Use a combination of gestures and words.
  √ Show children what you want them to do.

- **Use physical guidance to keep children safe.** Keep dangerous materials out of reach so that there are fewer occasions to have to redirect them. Temporarily separate children who are hurting each other.

## Responding to Children's Most Challenging Behaviors

### Temper Tantrums

There is no mistaking the red face, flailing limbs, and screaming that signal a young child's temper tantrum. Such outbursts result from the toddlers' lack of skill in dealing with anger and frustration.

*Frustration Tantrums* The best way to deal with a tantrum that comes from frustration is to change the conditions that are prompting the child's intense feelings. Replacing a puzzle that is too difficult, helping with snaps that won't close easily, removing the tricycle that constantly tips over, or adding more toys to the water table are all ways to ease frustrating situations.

*Anger Tantrums* The adult's approach changes when it seems that a child is using a tantrum to express anger over not getting his way. It is best to ignore such outbursts while they occur, because giving attention during the tantrum may reward the behavior, encouraging future repetitions. Once an angry tantrum has subsided, the teacher should provide positive attention, soothing the child or helping him approach the problem situation in a more constructive way. For example, after a tantrum about who has the truck, say, "Well, now you've stopped crying. Let's go look for the tractor."

## Toddler Negativism

Sometimes toddlers do the opposite of what adults request or shout "No!' as a way of declaring their autonomy leading to unnecessary power struggles between young children and teachers. Caregivers can use three strategies to avoid these negative outcomes:

- **Avoid issuing ultimatums to children.** Instead of saying, "Pick up those toys!" say, "Where do you think this toy could go?" or "Do you think the doll should go in the bed or on the chair?" Such statements give children a say in what is happening and make it easier for them to respond positively.

- **Offer children choices.** Toddlers are seeking real ways to exert power. Making a decision about which socks to wear, what color paper to use, or whether to start with a bite of rice or a taste of squash gives them an opportunity to "be in charge." Giving children a choice between two positive outcomes is a good way to help them feel successful and practice exerting power in constructive ways.

- **When children say no, pause before responding.** Avoid confronting children immediately. Try substitution or redirection instead. A brief pause gives children a chance to recompose themselves so that a second try may be met with less resistance.

## Biting

Biting is common behavior among infants and toddlers. Because it is so harmful, it cannot be tolerated and appropriate action must be taken the very first time a child bites and every time thereafter. According to the National Association for the Education of Young Children, children bite for several reasons:

- ***Some children are experimental biters.*** They use biting as a way to explore the environment. When an infant or toddler bites in an experimental way, say "No" in a firm voice. Explain that biting hurts and that the child may not bite. Offer the child a substitute object such as a teething ring.

- ***Some children bite out of frustration.*** They resort to biting when they cannot achieve their aims any other way or express their needs adequately. The child who wants a toy but doesn't have the words to get it, or a child who is frustrated because his tower keeps falling down may bite someone to establish rights or express frustration.

  If this happens, attend to the victim immediately. Tell the biter in a firm, calm voice that biting hurts and she may not bite. Teach children the words they need to communicate their needs and feelings to others. Use the strategies that are outlined in Chapter 4 for helping children express their emotions. Make sure to give frustrated biters positive attention when they practice new skills. Watch for situations in which a child's frustration is increasing and intervene *before* a bite occurs.

- **Some children bite because they feel threatened.** They bite in self-defense. These youngsters may be overwhelmed by the environment or may lack the skills they need to establish their rights in more productive ways.

  If a child bites for this reason, follow the procedures outlined above. In addition, use the logical consequence of having the biter soothe the victim in some way such as getting a wet towel or bandage to put on the bite. Help threatened biters learn words to defend their rights: "I'm not done," or "Wait," or "You can have it next." If a child seems overwhelmed, limit the number of children in an activity area, remove some materials, lessen the noise, or reduce the brightness of the lights. Any of these factors may overstimulate a child, making him less able to cope.

- **Some children bite to show power.** These children have such strong needs for autonomy and control that they find biting a rewarding way to gain attention. In addition to attending to the victim, and making it clear that biting is not allowed, give power biters opportunities to exert appropriate power throughout the day. Making choices, helping in the classroom, and gaining attention from other positive acts are appropriate ways to exert power.

*It is never appropriate to physically punish children or shame them in any way.* Such tactics teach children that physical force is an appropriate way to handle problems and concerns. Children then learn that "bigger" people can hurt other people to force them to do something or stop doing something. These are not desirable lessons for children to learn. Work with parents and other staff to consistently monitor children's challenging behaviors and provide children with alternate strategies to express their needs and desires.

## Conclusion

The most important lesson that infants and toddlers can learn is that they are worth loving. From the beginning, children must feel loved and valued. Even while they know that a specific behavior is not accepted, they absorb the message that they are worth loving. It is then a short step to the development of the notion that others, too, are valuable and also worth caring for. Responsive, sensitive caregiving in the early years prepares children for responsive, flexible relations with peers throughout life.

# CHAPTER 6

# GUIDING COGNITIVE DEVELOPMENT

# 6. GUIDING COGNITIVE DEVELOPMENT

Since early brain development is profoundly affected by the caregiving environment, parents and caregivers have a central role to play in providing the kinds of early experiences necessary for optimal development. This chapter is intended to help caregivers promote the cognitive development of the children in their care. It identifies the most important cognitive achievements of the infant and toddler period, tells what caregiving practices and behaviors are essential to cognitive development, and suggests activities that foster cognitive growth. It also provides a brief summary of toys, games, and other materials that support cognitive development.

## Important Cognitive Achievements

Infants and toddlers are constantly investigating the objects around them. They learn about them by touching, tasting, smelling, and listening. They test many characteristics of an object and learn as much from what does not work as from what does. They learn to generalize about the relationships they discover between objects and between actions and objects. Caregivers must understand the sequences and stages of cognitive development so they can support this early learning.

### Objects Are Permanent

Between six and nine months of age, infants begin to learn that objects are permanent and do not disappear when they are no longer in view. This includes beloved parents and caregivers and helps to explain a child's increasing concern for his mother to return.

### Imitation

Even in the earliest weeks of life, an infant will imitate his caregivers' facial expressions and actions: sticking out his tongue or wrinkling his eyebrows. Toddlers learn how to do things by imitating more complex actions: trying to change a doll's diaper or feeding the teddy bear.

### Making Interesting Experiences Continue

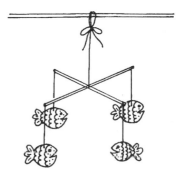

When a child is about four-months old, he learns how to make interesting experiences continue. He might accidentally kick a mobile, causing the colorful object to move or jingle. By repeating the kicking motion, the baby continues the experience. Infants learn that they can kick their legs, wave their arms, and shake and rub objects to continue accidentally discovered, but very interesting experiences.

## Intentional Actions

Between 5 and 12 months of age, infants begin to use their bodies intentionally to manipulate objects. They begin by reaching. Later, they use problem-solving techniques like using a stick to get a toy. They also begin to learn what certain action sequences mean: for instance, when a caregiver begins to open jars and get the spoons, it is almost time to eat. Caregivers help to build these skills by talking about what they are doing: "See the carrots? Here is a spoon. It is almost lunch time."

## Cause and Effect

Infants and toddlers also begin to learn how actions fit together to produce a result. Mobile infants learn that they can pull a string attached to an interesting toy in order to get the toy. Gradually, they learn to repeat increasingly complicated actions. At around 15 months of age, infants begin to search for causes. For instance, they are curious about what makes a light go off and on or why a toy makes an interesting sound, and will investigate tirelessly to find what causes something to happen.

## Spatial Relationships

Young infants do not understand concepts like distance, size, and space, but as they become mobile, they learn about these relationships through experience. Slowly but inevitably, infants learn about spatial relationships as they bump into walls, crawl under tables and then cannot get out, and reach for interesting toys they cannot possibly grasp. Caregivers can help by identifying spatial relationships and detours. For instance, when an infant is about to crawl into a shelf, the caregiver might say, "Gina, crawl *around* the shelf," while motioning the action.

## Mastery Motivation

From the time they first learn to repeat actions, infants and toddlers demonstrate an intense desire to master an action by trying it over and over again or by trying different actions until the task is solved. This is called mastery motivation. As they progress from infancy to toddlerhood, the number of repetitions increases and the activities become more complicated.

## Polar Concepts

Mobile infants and toddlers begin to learn about relative attributes as they discover polar concepts (opposites or extremes), like "big" and "little," "hot" and "cold," or "dark" and "light," long before they understand "medium," "warm," or shades of gray.

## *Caregiver Qualities and Behaviors Essential to Children's Cognitive Development*

As they interact with a responsive world, infants and toddlers learn that their actions can affect what happens. They also tend to share their discoveries and triumphs with beloved caregivers. Consequently, caregivers have an extraordinary influence on children's cognitive development.

A responsive caregiver promotes a child's cognitive development when she encourages him to act and engages him in talking about what he is doing. For example, as a child takes blocks from a shelf, the caregiver asks what the child is building and remarks on the placement of the blocks, praises the child's efforts, and asks whether or where or why the caregiver should place a block. On the other hand, a caregiver who takes down the blocks herself, says, "Let's build a castle," tells the child to hand her the blocks, and directs the child to put blocks in certain places, has hindered the child's cognitive development.

Caregivers who promote and support children's cognitive development share five essential behaviors:

- They are responsive.
- They are sensitive.
- They are partners in play.
- They encourage exploration while providing a safe base.
- They help children acquire a sense of mastery.

## Responsiveness

One of the key components of promoting children's optimal development is responsive caregiving. Responsiveness has three elements: contingency, appropriateness, and promptness.

> **Contingency** means that the caregiver's actions occur in response to the infant's action. If an infant coos with joy at the sight of his caregiver, the responsive caregiver responds by cooing in return.

***Appropriateness*** refers to the match between the caregiver's response and the child's action. Is the caregiver's response related to the baby's actions? In the example above, the caregiver's cooing response was conceptually related to the baby's actions. When the baby cooed, the caregiver did not respond by jiggling the infant's arms and legs. She gave a meaningful response.

***Promptness*** refers to the length of time between the infant's actions and the caregiver's response. In order for the infant to learn to associate her actions with the caregiver's response, the caregiver must act soon after the infant's behavior.

## Sensitivity

Sensitive caregivers are alert to each child's basic temperament, her present stage or developmental level, and mood or behavioral state.

***Temperament*** Sensitive caregivers are attuned to the individual characteristics of each child and understand how those characteristics relate to development. They come to understand the varying temperaments of the children for whom they care and they tailor their actions according to the children's individual temperaments. For example:

> *Jack seems wary of new experiences. He stays away from the new climber and settles himself with familiar books.*

The sensitive caregiver uses different approaches to promote the cognitive development of each child. Jack's caregiver places familiar toys near the new climber. When Jack approaches the climber to get a favorite toy, he is exposed to it in a non-threatening way. Gradually, he overcomes his reluctance and begins to explore the new climber.

***Developmental Levels*** Sensitive caregivers are good at matching a baby's skills with appropriate activities.

*Thirteen-month-old Emma is playing "Find the Hidden Toy" with Sonia, her caregiver. Emma watches as Sonia puts a favorite small toy into a cup and then shakes the toy out of the cup and under a cloth. Now the toy is hidden under the cloth.*

Sonia observes that Emma is having a hard time finding the toy. She simplifies the game by putting a larger toy under the cloth. A caregiver makes an activity more difficult to challenge one child, but simplifies the same activity for another child. Both children are working on the same skills, but at different levels. Each child will be successful in the task.

***Infant and Toddler Cues*** A baby's mood or behavioral state determines his receptivity to stimulation. The sensitive caregiver learns how to "read" a baby's cues. She recognizes the six infant behavioral states: active alert awake, quiet alert awake, crying, drowsy, active sleep, and quiet sleep. She knows that the best time to interact with a baby is when he is in the quiet alert state, when the baby is most focused on the caregiver's attempts to interact. The responsive caregiver also knows that tense body movements mean an infant needs to be soothed, not stimulated. The caregiver reads a child's cues to learn what his needs are at that moment and responds accordingly.

## Floor Time: "Partners in Play"

Caregivers promote cognitive development when they are actively involved with infants and toddlers at the children's level, literally down on the floor with them. This is one of the most important elements in a child-centered, rather than teacher-directed, setting. The caregiver is a facilitator and collaborator.

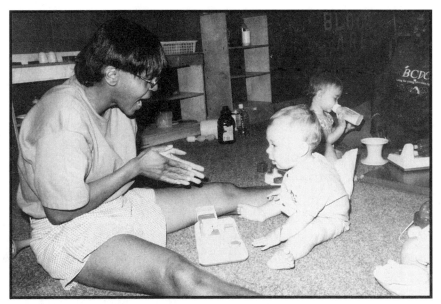

## A Safe Base: Encouraging Exploration

Infants and toddlers who have formed loving relationships with adults feel confident enough to risk venturing out to explore their worlds. They perceive their caregivers as "safe bases" to which they can return when they need the encouragement of a reassuring smile or a word of support.

## Promoting a Sense of Mastery

Infants and toddlers learn by trial and error. They investigate materials in detail, sometimes going back to the same activity day after day to experiment. When a child experiments and explores in her own time and her own way, her discoveries belong to her. She feels the excitement and joy in figuring out a problem. She feels a sense of mastery. Sensitive caregivers support children's explorations with activities suited to the developmental level of the child and, always, with encouraging words and smiles. When a child is slow to complete a task or solve a problem, the adult may be tempted to do it for him. She may want to finish the puzzle or make the jack-in-the-box pop up, but "helping" in this way does little to promote a child's cognitive development.

## *Activities That Foster Cognitive Development*

This section offers materials and activities that foster cognitive development. We do not suggest in any great detail *how* they should be used, because the best, most pertinent ideas will come from an infant or toddler at play.

## Problem-solving Activities

Infants' problem-solving skills are evident early in life. The three-month-old who turns her eyes and head to locate a hidden sound is demonstrating problem-solving skills, as is the five-month-old who can find a toy partially hidden under a cloth. Caregivers can help children  develop their problem-solving skills by presenting them with intriguing "problems." For example, offer a wooden cube to a seven-month-old who already has a cube in each hand. How will she solve this problem? Will she drop one cube to hold the third cube? Will she put a cube in her mouth so she can hold the third cube in her hand?

> ***Block Play*** Blocks (foam or plastic) give children opportunities to solve problems. As a child learns how to balance and stack one block on top of another, she is learning about spatial relationships.

***Empty and Fill Games*** Young children also use empty and fill games to practice problem solving. For example, after dropping the clothes pins through a slit cut in the top of the lid, the child is faced with the challenge of how to get them out again.

Other good materials for problem-solving practice include shape sorters, stacking rings, nesting cups, and puzzles for toddlers.

***"Tools"*** Children solve problems when they begin to use "tools" to help them accomplish tasks. The toddler who pulls a string attached to a toy to bring the toy closer is using problem-solving skills.

## Pretend Play

Pretend play helps toddlers build cognitive skills. Pretend play skills are first evident when toddlers begin to use common objects in place of other familiar objects. For example, a toddler might use a stick as a spoon to stir sand in a bucket or wear a bowl over his head as a hat. An infant and toddler program should have a pretend play area and many props that appeal to boys and girls alike.

## Sensory Experiences

Because infants and toddlers learn about their world through their senses, caregivers should provide a variety of sensory experiences.

***Sand Play*** Indoor and outdoor sandboxes provide exciting learning opportunities for toddlers. They love the scratchy feel of the sand in their hands or under their feet! Provide scoops and cups so they can practice skills like scooping, pouring, lifting, and digging. Sand play also helps children learn polar opposite concepts like "rough" and "smooth." Talk about the rough sand and the smooth side of the tub.

**Water Play** helps children learn concepts like "wet" and "dry." Provide a plastic tub of cold water and another of warm water and let children test "warm" and "cold." Toddlers can also practice pouring skills and, as they pour water from one container into another of a different size, begin to understand measurement concepts.

**Textures** Even young infants can learn from exposure to materials of varying textures. Place a carpet square, a silky scarf, and a rubber bath mat on the floor. As infants crawl or walk over the materials, caregivers describe the textures. Older children enjoy working with playdough. Let toddlers help to make no-cook playdough, using this recipe:

---

### RECIPE FOR NO-COOK PLAYDOUGH

- 12 parts flour
- 6 parts salt
- 1 part oil
- 4 parts water
- food coloring (optional)

Mix ingredients in a bowl with a spoon or by hand.

---

**Creative Expression** Art supplies, like extra-large crayons, non-toxic finger-paints and poster paints, large brushes, large sheets of paper, and playdough, promote toddler's development in two ways: they provide sensory experiences and opportunities for children to express themselves. Tearing paper also provides an interesting tactile and auditory experience.

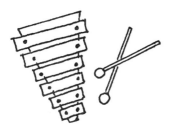

**Musical instruments** Bells, rattles, and drums provide pleasurable sensory experience for infants and toddlers. Even very young infants can swing a rattle or kick bells to produce a pleasurable sound. Older infants and toddlers enjoy pounding on drums.

## Early "Science" Experiences

Infants and toddlers are constantly engaging in "scientific experiments." They use trial and error and observation techniques daily. Caregivers can reinforce these efforts in a variety of ways. For example, adding a bucket of water to the sandbox illustrates cause and effect in a practical, easily demonstrable way. Similarly, adding water to dirt creates a new substance: it makes mud. And, in both experiments, children also learn about *wet* and *dry*.

## Helping Activities

Including toddlers in meaningful, daily life activities provides rich cognitive experiences. When toddlers help caregivers put away clean laundry (bibs, towels, blankets), they are learning how to sort. Toddlers enjoy helping to wash toys and plastic dishes, and learn concepts like *wet* and *dry*, *clean* and *dirty* at the same time.

## Cooking Experiences

Include children in simple cooking experiences like mixing muffin dough. Cooking activities teach cause and effect relationships (add water to flour and the consistency changes), provide measuring opportunities (important to later pre-math skills), and provide lots of opportunity for language development.

## Outdoor Experiences

*Plant a garden.* This activity encourages children to explore their natural world and introduces them to cognitive concepts, like sequencing: first, dig a hole, then add a seed, next cover the seed with soil, now water it carefully, . . . and watch it grow!

*Hang a bird feeder.* Children are fascinated by birds. As they observe birds at the feeder, children learn how and what various birds eat, how they relate to each other and how they fly. They can compare sizes and colors and listen to the different bird songs.

*Hang wind chimes.* In addition to sounding pleasant, the chimes and wind demonstrate a cause and effect relationship.

## *Reinforcing Cognitive Concepts With Language*

When caregivers talk with young children, they are using language to reinforce cognitive development. (Chapter 7, *Guiding Early Language Development*, explains the importance of language in fostering cognitive development.) Experienced caregivers recommend using the following techniques when talking with young children:

**Open-ended questions** are very effective with toddlers. Unlike questions that can be answered "yes" or "no" (Do you like this?) or with an answer that is either right or wrong (What color is this?), open-ended questions can be answered in many ways. "What will happen now?," "How did you do that?," and "What do you see?" are examples of open-ended questions.

**Provide explanations.** Using simple, descriptive language to explain things helps children as they build mental concepts.

> *Ethan holds a bucket of beads and then turns over the bucket. His eyes widen when the beads spill onto the floor. His caregiver explains, "You turned the bucket **over** and the beads fell **out**. You poured the beads **out**."*

Ethan's caregiver is using language to help him identify the cause and effect nature of his actions. Explanations should be clear, concise, and used in the context of the situation. As children gain more language skills, caregivers should begin to use more open-ended questions and statements. For instance, as Ethan's language skills grow, his caregiver might say, "What happened?" to encourage him to put words to his actions.

**Social Games** Social games provide cognitive and language experiences. Games like "Pat-a-Cake" call for turn-taking and sequencing skills. "Peek-a-Boo" is an amusing activity that gives infants practice with the concept of object permanence. Repeatedly playing "Hide-and-Seek" with a parent helps a child learn that her parent will not disappear forever. Most children love "Peek-a-Boo" and will initiate the game with adults. Their self-esteem and confidence is strengthened when an adult responds by joining the game.

## *Games and Materials That Promote Cognitive Development*

### Home-made Games and Materials

Expensive toys are not necessary for stimulating experiences. A child is learning about her world when she plays with ordinary everyday materials. Cardboard tubes can be used in a number of ways: looking through the tube, dropping objects through the tube, and blowing in the tube.

Ordinary household materials can be wonderful items for exploration. These include: cups, scoops, sifters, funnels, basters, cloth scraps, juice can lids, rug and carpet scraps, paper blocks made from paper milk and juice cartons, empty cardboard boxes, cardboard tubes, non-breakable mirrors, pots and pans, different sizes of plastic containers that can fit inside each other, and paper egg cartons.

Cups, sifters, and scoops are appropriate materials for a sand or water table. Plastic containers of different sizes can be used for nesting or sorting activities. Color the bottoms of egg carton cups and use them for color matching activities. Older toddlers can sort plastic bottle caps by color. The caps can also be used for dumping and filling games. Cut a slit in the plastic lid of a container and let children practice pushing craft sticks through the slit. Children can crawl in, through, or around cardboard boxes or use them for a variety of activities.

## Commercial Toys and Materials

Greenman and Stonehouse offer the following tips for choosing appropriate toys, games, and materials for infants and toddlers:

---

**TIPS FOR CHOOSING TOYS FOR INFANTS AND TODDLERS**

Choose:

- Toys that are durable
- Toys that engage many of a child's senses
- Toys that the child can "act on" instead of watching
- Toys that have interesting causal mechanisms (such as a jack-in-the-box)
- Toys that have logical, natural responses to causal mechanisms   (For example, a bell that rings is more logical than an electronic buzzer.)
- Toys that are adaptable to a wide range of developmental skills

---

## A Closing Thought

Infants and toddlers will learn no matter what.  The goal is to help them learn what is relevant to their development with efficiency, with a sense of accomplishment, and with joy.

# CHAPTER 7

# GUIDING EARLY LANGUAGE DEVELOPMENT

# 7. GUIDING EARLY LANGUAGE DEVELOPMENT

Language, more than any other ability, sets humans apart. It is almost impossible to stop a child from learning language. Which language she will learn and how useful it will be as a tool for thinking and communicating have their beginnings in these early years. This chapter discusses the stages of language development, strategies that promote language development, specific activities that support language, behaviors that promote early language development, and the physical environment that supports language acquisition.

## The Stages of Language Development

Language begins before birth. Infants are born preferring the voice of a special adult over the voice of a stranger. Long before any words are spoken, infants and toddlers communicate through their facial expressions, body movements, coos, and cries. As very young children learn to communicate successfully with their parents and care-givers, they come to recognize the power of language to make things happen. They quickly learn the basic pattern of language: agent, action, object. They use first one word, then two, then three to convey an entire idea. Thus, what is later "Mommy, I want some milk now," begins first as "milk," next "more milk," then "Jamie want milk," and so forth. When toddlers begin to formulate questions, sometime between 18 months and two years of age, they experiment with language by asking many questions. They also realize that if they ask a question, they are likely to capture the attention and get a response from an attentive adult.

When observing infants' and toddlers' communication behaviors, caregivers should be aware of the wide range in the speed of normal development, even though the sequence is the same. Every child passes through the same stages—first cooing, next babbling, and then one-word utterances—but with great variation. One infant may use one-word utterances at 10 months of age, whereas another child may not use single word speech until 18 months; both are within the developmentally normal range. For caregivers, this wide range means tailoring interactions and language modeling to the developmental readiness of each child.

Children understand spoken language (receptive language) before they can use it (expressive language). Receptive language is a prerequisite to expressive language. A child understands "Point to the dog," before she can say, "See doggie." (Adults who attempt to learn a new language recognize this sequence.) Infants and toddlers learn language by hearing it and speaking it. The process is greatly enhanced when adults encourage and support children's efforts to express themselves.

## *Strategies That Promote Language Development*

### Speaking Slowly and Clearly

Speaking slowly gives the young child time to process mentally the words she is hearing, and clear speech allows her to identify new words.

### Turn Taking

Some of the earliest conversations between infants and their caregivers contain no words at all. Infants and their special adults "talk" through facial expressions as they gaze at and study each other. Later, as infants begin to coo, the conversation includes rounds of the baby cooing and the caregiver's imitative responses with both the caregiver and baby pausing to let the other respond. The conversational turn taking continues as the baby begins to babble and use jargon.

Sometimes caregivers respond to a baby's "Bababa dadda ba" babble as if it has great meaning by saying "I hear you!" or "Is that so?" The caregiver's loving, enthusiastic intonation encourages the baby to continue babbling.

### Parallel Talk and Labeling Objects

When the caregiver puts words to the child's perceptions and actions, she is using parallel talk to help the child learn new words. Sitting near a toddler staring at a bird in an outside tree, the caregiver says, "You see the bird?" or "There's a bird!" Alert caregivers use parallel talk to capture the child's interest at the moment. As a toddler is turning the handle of a jack-in-the-box, a caregiver repeats, "Turn the handle, turn the handle." As an infant is crawling over a pillow, the caregiver might say, "Alex crawls *over* the pillow." Trying to "teach" toddlers new words by drill will leave both the child and caregiver frustrated. However, when infants and toddlers are surrounded by language in connection with their own activities, their vocabularies grow quickly.

Ethan tries to put the triangle in the square hole. He turns and turns it to try to make it go through. It won't. Then he sees the triangular hole and tries that one. Slowly, turning it, he finds the fit so it will fall through. His caregiver explains, "You found the hole that matches, and then you could push it through!"

### Expansion and Extension

When older infants and toddlers begin to use one- or two-word speech, caregivers expand what they are saying. If a 13-month-old says, "Ball," the caregiver might expand that word into a phrase or sentence, such as "There is the ball." This suggests a further step: "There's the big red ball." As toddlers begin to put more words together, adults provide more semantic or meaningful information to the child. For instance, if the toddler says, "That doggie," a caregiver might extend the thought with "Yes, the doggie has brown fur."

## Explaining Why

We use language all the time to tell children what we need to do next, be it lunch, naptime, diaper change, or getting dressed. Children begin to understand and remember to do something when these directions explain *why* we are doing it. When we give reasons for activities, even to the youngest children, we help to focus them and give them an interest in the activity at hand. When children hear suggestions like "We'll have to stop and clean up so we can get ready to go outside," they are receiving important messages about planning, persistence, self-regulation, and task completion.

## Open-Ended Questions and Responses

Unlike questions that can be answered with "yes" or "no," open-ended questions encourage a number of answers and foster language and cognitive growth. Imagine a toddler and her caregiver on the playground. The toddler, pointing at a tree, asks the caregiver, "What's that?" In response, the caregiver asks, "What do you see?" thus giving the toddler opportunity to talk about the leaves, the bird in the tree, or the squirrels chasing each other around the tree trunk.

Open-ended questions also encourage the child to begin thinking about herself as a person. For example, by asking "Who is laughing?" the caregiver is helping the child be aware of what she is doing.

Open-ended questions and responses build conversation skills. A child comments, the caregiver encourages further speech by using an open-ended question or response, and the child has the opportunity to answer. Extended conversations between toddlers and caregivers are related to later language competence.

## Scaffolding

Infant caregivers use favorite games such as "Pat-a-Cake" as "scaffolds" to teach language. For example, at first, the baby may be a passive participant in the game of "Pat-a-Cake". Obviously, if the child shows no interest or is focused on something else, the caregiver waits until another time, but if she is interested the caregiver encourages her to be a more active participant. The caregiver waits for the baby to move her hands in motion, omitting a word in the rhyme for the baby to fill in with a vocalization. Because the caregiver has used a game as a learning situation or as a *scaffold*, the baby begins to understand more about how to communicate.

With a toddler, the caregiver might prompt the child. For instance, she might leave out the last word in a familiar nursery rhyme for the toddler to complete. In reading a story about pets, the caregiver might say, "I see a big, furry . . . " and encourage the toddler to fill in the missing word, "dog." As the child's language skills increase, the prompt will no longer be needed.

Language helps develop a child's memory. The caregiver who says, "Yesterday we had spaghetti for lunch," is helping cement the words and the past experience in children's minds.

## Using Language in Daily Routines

Daily routines such as diaper changes and meal times are good moments to develop language skills. Children can name common items like cup, fork, apple, and table. Use precise terms rather than general ones: "This yogurt is creamy. It's sweet," or "What a crunchy cracker!" Saying "Good for you! You can hold your *cup*!" rather than "Good for you! You can hold *it*!" teaches the meanings of new words.

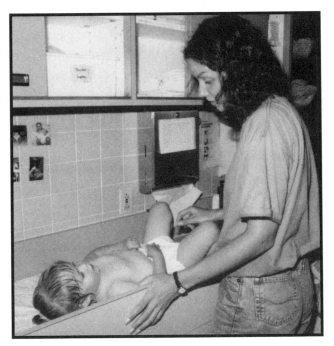

Diaper changing is a particularly good time for one-to-one communication because the caregiver is focused exclusively on one child. (See Chapter 9, *Using Daily Routines as Learning Experiences*, for a detailed discussion of how to use diapering routines as learning experiences.)

## *Activities That Promote Early Language Development*

### Reading and Looking at Books

Reading to children may be the single most important activity in supporting their language development. It allows them to hear new and unfamiliar words when they are acutely focused and enjoying a warm relationship with the reader. Children should be read to every day. Infants and toddlers love to finger books, turning pages and being "surprised" at the pictures. From their earliest months, infants enjoy being held and read to. The sound of a caregiver's familiar voice calms and soothes them. They feel nurtured and loved while held during this special time with a caregiver. Reading each page of a book is not important. They can look at the colorful pictures in the book. Encourage children to look at, handle, and even taste books that are hard to destroy. Books should be displayed and accessible for children to pick up on their own.

When caregivers read slowly, infants and toddlers can enjoy the sounds of language. A child who is engrossed in a colorful picture of a dog may not be ready to go on to the next page, so the caregiver must be sensitive to his interests and follow his cues. A sensitive caregiver notices an infant's interest in the picture of the dog and says cheerfully, "A dog." With a toddler, she uses more words, "You see the dog, " or asks the child, "What do you see?" Finishing the book is not as important as the child's leisurely exploration of the book, and toddlers love to hear the same story over and over again.

---

**TIPS FOR CHOOSING BOOKS FOR INFANTS**

- *Choose books with thick pages* that are easy to turn and hard to tear.
- *Choose books that are durable and easy to clean.* Since infants explore books by mouthing, choose books made of cloth, soft vinyl, or plastic and which are easy to wash.
- *Choose some "things to do" books* with flaps that open and close to reveal hidden pictures.
- *Choose books with clear, simple photographs of familiar objects* so that children can practice naming animals, clothing, food, etc.
- *Choose books that have one picture and one word per page.* Too much detail is confusing.

---

```
┌─────────────────────────────────────────────────────────────┐
│                                                               │
│           TIPS FOR CHOOSING BOOKS FOR TODDLERS                │
│                                                               │
│     •  Choose books that are short.                           │
│     •  Choose books with clear, simple pictures.              │
│     •  Choose books they can handle easily without tearing pages. │
│     •  Choose books with predictable endings.                 │
│     •  Choose stories with repetition.                        │
│     •  Choose "things to do" books.                           │
│     •  Choose rhyming stories.                                │
│     •  Make a book of the children's photographs.             │
│     •  Choose books that show people of all ages, genders, and │
│        cultures.                                              │
│                                                               │
└─────────────────────────────────────────────────────────────┘
```

## Chanting and Singing

Most young children enjoy music, and singing with infants and toddlers builds a love of language. Using chants at lunch time, such as "Lunch time, lunch time. Now it is lunch time," helps to calm hungry children as well as demonstrate that language has purpose, and can be fun.

Infants and toddlers love the cadence of nursery rhymes and other poems set to simple melodies. Make up a simple tune or borrow a tune from a favorite song.

## "Hands-on" Activities

As a child plays—touching, holding, or sorting objects—talk to her about what she is doing. A toddler learns the meaning of cold by touching snow and the meaning of wet by playing at the water table or going out in the rain. Young children's active play affords caregivers many opportunities to extend the acquisition of language:

**Matching Games** Use plastic bowls or color the cups of an egg carton to make a color matching game. Start with just a few colors like red, yellow, and blue. As toddlers put colored cubes or beads into the matching colored cups, talk about what they are doing: "Katie is putting a red bead in the red cup."

**A "Feely Box"** Make a "feely box" out of common items like cotton balls and a piece of sandpaper. As the child examines the objects, first identify the objects as "cotton" and "sandpaper" and then describe them as "soft" or "scratchy." As time goes by, add other objects.

***Waterplay*** Waterplay attaches new concepts and new words, like pour, drip, and splash. Help a toddler learn what drip means by punching a hole in the bottom of a plastic container. Provide materials such as measuring cups and scoops, plastic containers, funnels, and spoons in the water table.

(See Chapter 6 for a detailed description of activities that promote both cognitive and language development.)

## Behaviors That Promote Early Language Development

### Model correct language.

When responding to the children, caregivers should accept the children's language even with conceptual or grammatical mistakes, while modeling correct language. On their own and in time, children will correct their mistakes if they hear proper language around them. An older toddler might overgeneralize the concept of dog and call any furry animal with legs "dog." Without actually telling the child she made a mistake, caregivers can refer to it as a cat. Similarly, if a child says, "Matthew hitted Maria," simply say, "Did Matthew hit Maria?" rather than correcting him.

### Always respond to children's questions.

As toddlers are learning language, they often stay close to their caregivers, ask questions like "What's that?," bring objects to caregivers to label, and carefully watch the caregiver's mouth as she speaks. To a busy caregiver, these behaviors may seem frustrating. However, a caregiver's patient and sensitive response is vital in the language learning process. Emma, an inquisitive toddler twice asks, "What is that?" as her caregiver wipes the breakfast table. The caregiver responds, "You see my cloth. I'm wiping the food off the table. Wipe, wipe, wipe," and models language that helps Emma to understand what "wipe" means and what "off" means. Then, giving a clean cloth to Emma, she puts language in action.

## Speak at the child's linguistic level.

Challenging and encouraging children is fine, but caregivers should remember to use clear, simple speech with infants and toddlers. Long sentences or multiple sentences together confuse toddlers who are trying both to understand language and decipher concepts.

## Do not rely on television to teach language.

For a child, there is no substitute for clear language that is relevant to what he is doing or looking at, and is directed straight at him from someone who cares about him. Language broadcast from television and the words of adults talking to each other cannot begin to replace one-to-one conversation with the child.

## *Creating a Language-rich Environment*

A language-rich environment includes both spoken language and print. Even though infants and toddlers cannot read, early exposure to *printed language*—not only books—promotes a future interest in literacy.

Label common objects such as table, chair, window, mirror, door, sink, and shelf, at the children's eye level. Calling special attention to the labels or trying to "teach" toddlers about the labels is not necessary.

Use a marker to outline an object on a shelf. Draw or paste a picture of a toy and label it. This visual cue helps toddlers to find and put away the toy independently and also builds language through the picture, the label and, later, through words.

Set up a "book corner." A book corner should be a relatively quiet and inviting place with a rocking chair or other comfortable spot for an adult to hold a child while reading to her.

## *Conclusion*

The infant and toddler center can be an excellent environment for children's language development, *if* caregivers understand and value ways to promote it. The consequences of not doing so can be serious. The rewards of doing so are significant: children who have a broad vocabulary, who can understand others and express themselves, and who believe what they say is valued and important. They will have a rich language base as they come of age in the 21st century.

# CHAPTER 8

# GUIDING PHYSICAL DEVELOPMENT

# 8. GUIDING PHYSICAL DEVELOPMENT

Physical development has two meanings.  One is growth in size.  This comes naturally to most children, depending upon good nutrition.  The second meaning, the subject of this chapter, is the increasing ability to use one's body purposefully to accomplish a variety of ends.  Muscle movement becomes ever more differentiated: the infant who responds by wriggling his whole body eventually becomes the adult with the ability to raise just one eyebrow at a time.  Much of childhood is devoted to this process of mastery through endless practice of gross motor activities like running, climbing, and jumping, and fine motor activities, like writing, grasping, or placing a puzzle piece.  (Appendix A, *Developmental Milestones of Children from Birth to Age 3*, shows the usual progression of physical development.)  This chapter discusses the caregiver's role in guiding physical development, individual differences in sensori-motor development, and activities that foster physical development.

## *The Role of the Caregiver*

The caregiver's role in guiding physical development is to provide a wide range of both large and small motor experiences that will encourage and support infants and toddlers as they begin to explore their physical surroundings.  Infants need to look at interesting

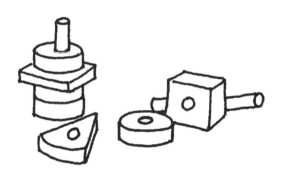

objects, reach, grab, hold, shake, and kick them, and have space to crawl.  Toddlers need plenty of space to push, pull, pick things up and put them down, walk, climb, jump, and run.  When caregivers provide a wide variety of motor experiences, infants and toddlers increase their repertoire of actions as well as their sense of pride and accomplishment.

When planning physical activities for young children, teachers must think about each child's skill level.  Before a child can learn a complex skill, he must learn prior, more basic skills.  For instance, before a toddler can scribble with a crayon, she has to have the finger control needed to hold the crayon.  Before a child can walk, he must crawl.  When caregivers understand the concept of prior basic skills, they are able to provide the most developmentally appropriate experiences for children.

## *Individual Differences in Sensori-motor Development*

When providing appropriate experiences for the motor development of infants and toddlers, caregivers must be sensitive to the individual differences in temperament that may cause some children to react negatively to new physical experiences. (See Chapter 2 for a discussion of individual differences.)

### Hypersensitivity

Hypersensitive children are easily overwhelmed by sights, sounds, or being touched, especially if the stimuli are very strong, sudden, or strange to the child.

> *Fifteen-month-old Sam is playing with his caregiver who is rolling new, brightly colored balls to him. Other children are playing with the balls too. As the noise and excitement level rises, Sam begins to cry. Soon, he is in the midst of a tantrum.*

Sam is a hypersensitive child, easily overwhelmed by noisy play. He expresses these feelings by crying, clinging, or "fussy" behavior. As a toddler, the extremely sensitive child may appear very cautious and fearful or have frequent tantrums. For overly sensitive children, new toys like brightly colored balls or body games like "Pat-a-Cake" may be overstimulating at first. In that case, a caregiver might assume mistakenly that Sam does not want to share toys. She might view him as greedy or jealous. Experienced caregivers, however, understand that these children need to be somewhat sheltered from too much excitement or to approach a task at a slower pace.

### Hyperactivity

Hyperactive children are always in motion and want a lot of physical sensory experiences. Unlike hypersensitive children, hyperactive children "underreact" to sensations of sight, sound, and touch, and consequently seek more sensory, visual, and tactile stimulation than the average child.

> *Eighteen-month-old Ana is constantly touching something! She grabs toy after toy from the shelf. She splashes at the water table, spilling water onto the floor. She hurls herself at her caregiver for a hug.*

Ana's caregiver understands her active, sometimes aggressive behavior. For active children like Ana, a combination of understanding and appropriate structure and rules help her manage and thrive in her environment. Her teacher might ask Ana to get something for her from across the room or to help another child who can't carry everything. She might be asked to choose a book or be given an extra hug.

# *Indoor Activities for Large Motor Development*

## Floor Time

Infants and toddlers need space and lots of time on the floor to stretch, reach, kick, roll, creep, crawl, and walk. By getting down on the floor with a child, a caregiver encourages him to explore the area. Even infants as young as two months are able to bear weight on their forearms and push up a little when lying on their stomachs. When a caregiver sits on the floor, at his level, talking to him, smiling, and encouraging him, the infant will push up to see the caregiver.

## Massaging and Stretching

Caregivers do not need special equipment to support the physical development of infants in their care. Gently massaging and stretching the baby's arms and legs makes the child aware of her body and exercises her muscles. While the baby lies on her back, gently bend her knees toward her stomach, and then gently straighten the legs out again. Talk cheerfully or sing and look into the baby's eyes while you exercise her muscles. This special one-on-one time is important to the child's emotional as well as physical development.

## Songs, Chants, and Music

Songs, chants, and music are used to promote body awareness and exercise muscles. Infants enjoy whirling around a room, safe and snug in the arms of a caregiver. As the caregiver moves the baby's arms in time to the music, they are both exercising large muscles. Toddlers will happily bob up and down to the steady, bouncing rhythm.

Infants and toddlers practice motor skills when they sing or move to songs that use hand or body movements. They love songs that have a surprise or call for a specific action that can be sung again and again, encouraging them to wait for the surprise or make the movement at the expected time.

## Fingerplays

Even simple games like playing with fingers promote physical development. Fingerplays give older infants and toddlers practice in isolating finger movements and moving their whole arms for both small muscle and large muscle development.

## Grasping and Manipulating Objects

Lightweight rattles, squeeze toys, and plastic grasping rings encourage infants to practice grasping and reaching skills. These are among the earliest large motor skills to develop; even very young babies will bat at toys hanging over their cribs.

By the age of three months, infants are beginning to reach toward toys although they cannot yet grasp and hold them. Place toys or rattles nearby so infants can practice reaching skills. Try to put a toy in an infant's hand so she can succeed in touching the item she sees. A caregiver's warm voice and enthusiastic smile encourages a baby to keep trying. By four months children can reach for objects and, by six months, they can reach across their bodies to grasp a toy on the opposite side.

Infants and toddlers practice "handling skills" in many ways as they learn to touch, grasp, hold, and manipulate materials. It is very important to have toys where children can reach for them as they choose. A mobile infant who successfully reaches for an object from a low shelf begins to realize how many choices he can make.

Between five and seven months, infants begin to transfer objects from one hand to the other hand. Provide hand-size wooden cubes or other lightweight objects so infants can practice this new skill. Caregivers should talk enthusiastically with infants about their new skills!

Between five and seven months, infants also learn to drop an object and then recover it. Dropping and recovering an object requires several skills. The child must learn to release the object, visually track the object, and then pick the object up. However, if the toy drops out of sight, the game is over! At this age, if an infant cannot see the toy, it does not exist. The patient caregiver must understand the joy of these newly discovered skills, even as a baby drops toy after toy!

## Pulling Up and Bearing Weight

From about six months, infants can pull themselves up to a standing position. Caregivers must be sure furniture is steady and will not tip over. At about the same age, an infant can bear weight on his legs and bounce. Between 6 and 10 months, the infant can stand if he holds onto furniture or an adult. This time is exciting for both child and adult. However, caregivers must not rush an infant to stand alone before he is ready. This is a time to applaud and encourage the baby's efforts but not to push him beyond his abilities. Some children are much more cautious than others.

## Crawling

Caregivers can encourage crawling skills by placing desirable toys just out of the infant's reach so she will have to crawl toward it. Encourage an infant by responding enthusiastically to his efforts and be alert to any signs of frustration. If the caregiver challenges the child while creating an environment in which he will be successful, the child will soon learn to crawl.

## Climbing

Crawling infants and toddlers like to climb low, soft structures approximately four to six inches above the floor. The structure should be wide enough to support the child's body without tipping and soft so that the baby doesn't get hurt. Climbers give children the opportunity to practice skills like spatial relationships, crawling, and climbing. Climbers with two or three low, wide stairs, rocking boats, and small slides are also useful. Toddlers love to practice walking on slight inclines or going up and down a single step.

## Walking

There is wide variation in the age at which infants begin to walk. Some babies may take their first steps at nine months, while other babies may not walk until many months later. This variation may be as much a matter of temperament as coordination. Do not push the child to walk. Letting a baby crawl and pull herself up allows her to learn the prior skills of balance and control of locomotion. In contrast, "walking" a baby across the floor by holding his hands while his feet drag along the floor is frustrating and confusing for the baby. As toddlers begin to walk, push and pull toys with handles (or strings no longer than 12 inches) provide opportunities to practice their newfound skills of upright mobility and balance.

## Balls

Balls are good toys for young children because they allow them to refine large motor skills like reaching, grasping, and letting go. They also learn about predicting the direction and speed of a moving object. Sit on the floor with an older infant and roll a ball back and forth. The ball should be lightweight and easy to grasp. At about 13 months of age, infants can throw a ball underhand.

## Lifting, Carrying, and Building Blocks

Soft blocks made of sturdy cardboard or cloth-covered foam make wonderful toys for toddlers to lift, carry, and build with on the floor. Younger toddlers focus not on building, but on exploring and investigating, and endlessly arranging and rearranging the individual blocks. Caregivers encourage this exploration by joyfully commenting on children's actions and playing with them on the floor. For older toddlers and two-year-olds, blocks are used to refine small motor coordination, learn about balance, and extend their imaginations as they begin symbolic play.

## *Indoor Activities for Small Muscle Development*

### Visual Focusing Skills

Pictures, photographs, and non-breakable mirrors provide interesting stimuli that increase infants' visual focusing skills. They should be hung low enough to be seen by infants who are not yet mobile. Mobiles also help to increase infants' visual focusing skills as well as their visual tracking skills.

## Moving, Pushing, Poking, and Turning

Beginning at about seven months of age, infants enjoy using both hands to explore objects. Activity boxes with things to move, push, poke, and turn are wonderful for practicing fine motor skills. Staff or families can make "activity boxes." Infants will keep busy playing with a slide lock, a light switch that clicks up and down, or a dial that turns, all securely fastened to a board. Toddlers will enjoy a busy board that includes a large zipper, large buttons sewn on fabric with matching large button holes, and a large, stiff string to thread through large holes.

## Pincer Grasp: Using Thumb and Forefinger

From about 10 months, an infant can use the thumb and forefinger to pick up objects in a pincer grasp. When a child begins to use a pincer grasp, he will enjoy picking up objects and finger foods like dry cereal. All hard objects accessible to the child should be too big to swallow.

## Pushing and Pulling

Large pop beads or toys that fit together encourage children to practice small motor skills like pulling. Balls or toys with wheels (hand-sized plastic cars, for example) that can be pushed across the floor give children practice in refining their large and small motor skills. Infants usually enjoy push and pull toys that provide interesting auditory or visual stimulation, such as a plastic car that makes clicking noises or a toy dog whose head bobs up and down. Most toddlers enjoy pushing a toy vacuum cleaner with beads that pop inside a plastic globe as they push.

Make empty-and-fill toys for infants and toddlers. Cut a slit in the plastic lid of a plastic container and let children push or poke wooden clothespins or large beads through the slit.

## Puzzles and Pegboards

As older infants and toddlers develop greater control over their fingers, give them puzzles with simple, large pieces. Pegboards are also useful for practicing small muscle skills.

## Playdough

Working with playdough involves both small and large muscles, as toddlers use all the muscles in the hand to squeeze, push, pull, and twist the playdough. Those who have a lot of upper body strength will use whole arm movements to bang, pat, and push the playdough.

## Coloring

Creative experiences using materials like paint, markers, and crayons also support small motor development as children learn to grasp and draw at the same time.

## *Outdoor Activities*

Both infants and toddlers benefit from outside play. During warm weather, spread a blanket on the ground in the shade for infants to enjoy the sights and sounds of the outdoors. Lay some toys on the blanket and incorporate fingerplays, songs, and chants with body movements for wonderful outside fun.

For toddlers, push-and-pull toys, like a play lawnmower provide many hours of play. Make sure that riding cars or other toys are low so that children can get on or off easily.

Start toddlers with toys they propel by "walking" on the ground before they advance to pedal-propelled vehicles. Riding toys strengthen large muscles and also present many opportunities to learn about spatial relationships and how to solve problems. The toddler who is driving a toy car must avoid obstacles in his path!

Large cardboard boxes turned on their sides make wonderful tunnels for crawling. Low outdoor climbers and small slides also provide ample opportunities for large motor exploration.

Children love to dig, scoop, pour, sift, and rake sand with shovels, water, and containers of various sizes. Sandbox play uses both large and small muscles.

Take advantage of items in the natural world. During autumn, collect colored leaves with children. In spring and summer, collect green leaves and dandelions. As they collect, the children will use large muscles to squat down and stand up. They will practice balancing and use small muscle skills as they visually locate a leaf to pick up and bring home. The outdoor world is full of opportunities for exploration.

## A Final Note

Infants and toddlers love to use their growing bodies as they begin to tame the world around them. Be sure they enjoy themselves as they use the experiences and equipment you provide.

# CHAPTER 9

# USING DAILY ROUTINES AS LEARNING EXPERIENCES

# 9. USING DAILY ROUTINES AS LEARNING EXPERIENCES

## Routine Activities Are Learning Experiences

Because so much of the young child's day is taken up with routine activities, they provide the context for the child's relationships and learning. Routines include ordinary activities like arriving, departing, feeding, diapering, dressing, bathing, storybook reading, and playing. Most routines are short, repeated frequently, and, in the case of infants and toddlers, require the support of a caregiving adult.

Part of infants' and toddlers' "sense of self" is built on the foundation of caregivers' responsiveness during these repeated daily routines and activities. Caregivers can use these as opportunities to nurture the individual needs of each child. This chapter explains how to use everyday routines as learning experiences that support children's emotional, cognitive, language, and physical needs.

## What Children Learn in Routines

### Young Infants

Young infants are at the mercy of their physical needs, more so than older children. Therefore, adults who consistently and predictably meet those needs set the foundation of trust and attachment.

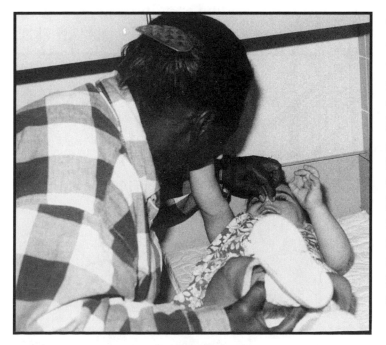

The predictability of routines at this early stage helps infants learn to anticipate and participate in interactions. As caregivers explain what is happening and what will happen next, the child is encouraged to participate and cooperate. Some babies prefer routine activity to be slow; others enjoy a more lively style. And, from time to time, they show that they are ready for a change. Therefore, routines, and the interactions that go with them, should be slightly different for each child.

Infants love to play simple interactive games. Diapering, dressing, and feeding provide times to play those little games together, or to hold and "talk" about some object of mutual attention. Even young infants practice simple turn-taking games, such as "Where's Una? There she is!" and soon learn to initiate them.

## Mobile Infants

Crawling and walking gives mobile infants a sense of control over their environment and their adult caretakers. Rolling, crawling, and walking transform an infant's routines into action-oriented experiences; as a consequence, caregivers have to be increasingly alert to the children's safety. This is also an age when children get easily frustrated, especially as they begin to practice self-help skills and routines. A child gets frustrated when she has to lie down for a diaper changing, or cannot remove her hat despite repeated tugging, or when the spoon misses her mouth and her food falls on the floor. Similarly, the mobile infant may signal to the caregiver that independence is essential one minute and assistance even more essential the next. Caregivers must balance the independence and support that crawlers and walkers need.

Caregivers must also find a balance between enough but not too much stimulation and exploration in their daily activities and routines. Routinely practicing skills throughout the day can be messy, upsetting, and tiring for children. Caregivers provide support in daily routines by making and maintaining eye contact, gesturing reassuringly, offering a gentle hand for guidance, and describing the actions to the child in short, grammatically correct phrases and sentences.

## Toddlers

Toddlers are learning to become more independent in feeding and dressing themselves as well as learning to share and cooperate with their peers. However, increasing sophistication does not come without challenges for the young child. For many children this age, learning means testing the limits of the caregivers and the environment, truly a personal test of the cause and effect relationship. When given a choice of two activities, they may want both at the same time or even one not being offered. A child may practice his emerging language skills in an attempt to persuade the caregiver to do what he wants or to protest the rules. On the other hand, toddlers are much better able to understand the reasons why a daily routine is important. They can also accept or suggest a variation that makes it more interesting.

## *Developing Individualized Routines Within the Daily Schedule*

The daily schedule is a guide, not a mandate. It is a framework for planning and organizing the daily routine and play activities. The schedule is developed by the staff, with family input. It considers many factors: the age of the children, the number of children to be served, developmental level and needs of individual children, and family preferences. Logistical considerations are also important: children's arrival and departure times, number of children at different times of the day, and the meal schedule. Keeping these and specific community and cultural considerations in mind, staff can establish general timelines for a daily schedule. A successful schedule is flexible and balanced.

### Flexibility and Balance

A flexible schedule supports young children in maintaining the general routines of the day when unforeseen events disrupt them. For example, families may arrive late because of bad weather. If the morning playtime extends from 8:00 to 10:00, children who are late can still have playtime after breakfast. Similarly, if the day turns out to be beautiful, a flexible schedule allows for a stroller ride to the park between meals and naptime.

Infants and toddlers need a balance between quiet and active times, between private and group play. Balance changes according to the child's development and temperament. In multi-age classrooms, balance can be a challenge because children of different ages have different needs. For example, young infants need more sleep than crawlers and toddlers. In turn, crawlers and toddlers may or may not need more sleep than walkers and runners. A flexible, balanced schedule will adapt to these differences with creative staffing. No one schedule will meet the needs of all children. Staff need to continuously observe the needs of individual children within the schedule's general guidelines. If most of the children seem suddenly tired, one teacher can begin naptime, while another reads quietly to other children not yet ready to rest.

## *Developing Curriculum Charts and Matrices*

For infants and toddlers, most schedules identify specific routines that occur at times throughout the day in a consistent and predictable order. Caregivers often view routines such as breakfast or lunch as tasks or duties to be completed rather than as part of the child's *curriculum*. When caregivers see routines as learning experiences, they can design individually focused learning opportunities within the routines. One way to begin the process of individualizing within routines and activities is to develop a Curriculum Chart. A Curriculum Chart is a visual display of the daily schedule of routines and activities. Similarly, caregivers may wish to set up a weekly Developmental

Matrix to show which learning opportunities might be built into routines. Several goals from different domains can easily be integrated into one routine. (See *Sample Daily Curriculum Chart* and *Sample Weekly Developmental Matrix* at the end of this chapter.)

## What to Teach in Routine Activities

The *Sample Developmental Goals Chart* at the end of this chapter lists some of the many abilities that can be fostered within the daily routine. The staff can use the chart at planning meetings to identify various skills and experiences for the children. Children should not be forced to complete the planned activities. These charts are more a *vision* in the teacher's mind than a blueprint for action on any particular day.

### Arrival and Departure Routines

Arrival and departure routines are critical to starting and ending the day well. Parents and caregivers work together to provide infants and toddlers with a safe, secure, and sensitive transition between home and center. They give parents and caregivers a chance to share information about a child and her day. It is just as important for the caregiver to know that the infant was awake and teething most of the night as it is for the parents to know that the child slept most of the day and woke up fussy. The adults might then alter or modify their schedules or their roles to adapt to the child's needs.

Caregivers play an important role during arrival and departure routines. When a caregiver greets each family individually each morning, she is helping to alleviate the separation anxiety that a parent and child may be feeling. In addition, if the caregiver greets the family each day, both child and family are reassured by the constancy of the routine. Departure times often have other challenges. An infant may not want to leave the comfort and security of being with a familiar caregiver at the end of the day. As a result, the infant may ignore the parent. A toddler may not want to stop playing because she is having fun. The toddler may become agitated and angry when taken away from the activity. The sensitive caregiver helps the child prepare for the transition, talking the child through the activity, and encouraging the parent to become involved. Time spent establishing and reestablishing relationships is well spent.

> *Tommy has waited for a chance to ride the kiddy car. Now it's free. Just as he gets on it, his mother arrives to take him home. The caregiver brings his mother over, saying, "Look at Tommy on the kiddy car!" His mother say, "Wow! That's almost like the one at home, Tommy. Hi, darling!" Tommy slides off and grabs her hand. After a short discussion about Tommy's day, they leave.*

## Feeding Routines

Feeding routines are scheduled at consistent and designated times. For young infants, the feeding schedule is based on individual eating patterns. Feeding times for the older children are usually set at designated times: for example, 8:00 a.m. for breakfast, 10:00 a.m. for a snack, and 11:30 a.m. for lunch, depending on what works best for the group. Feeding routines do more than provide nutritious meals. They can also strengthen the bond between caregiver and infant and enhance early communication as caregiver and child smile,

coo, and point back and forth. The skills that lead to independence and self-reliance are readily taught to children at mealtimes. For example, they learn to ask for things and practice fine motor skills as they pour milk and use utensils. Staff must remember that expectations about proper mealtime behaviors—for example, fingerfeeding, independent use of cups and utensils, and sharing food from a common bowl—vary significantly across communities and cultures. Consequently, it is important for families to participate in the identification of developmental skills for each child.

## Diapering and Toileting Routines

Few routines allow for prolonged one-to-one interactions with infants and toddlers as diapering, a time when the caregiver has a chance to have sustained eye contact and individual conversation with that child.

For older toddlers, toileting routines occur regularly throughout the day, giving them repeated opportunities to learn and practice self-help skills of dressing, undressing, and good hygiene. Family and caregivers should agree on their expectations for each child's toilet training, so that children do not get conflicting messages from the significant adults in their lives.

## Dressing and Undressing Routines

Dressing and undressing routines occur naturally throughout the day as children change for naptime or outdoors. Dressing and undressing routines encourage face-to-face interactions as a caregiver and infant play simple games like "Peek-a-Boo" or "This Little

Piggy" while the caregiver puts a sock on the baby. Undressing is easier for crawlers and toddlers and they often create their own opportunities when you least expect it! Dressing and undressing routines give toddlers repeated opportunities to:

- Gain independence as they practice their new self-help skills
- Watch other children dress themselves and begin to imitate those motions
- Follow simple directions
- Practice sequencing—the sock goes on before the shoe

## *Individualizing Routines*

The caregiver begins the individualization process by observing a child and identifying reasonable expectations for that child's routines. The expectations are based on two factors: the child's current skills and interest and the family's priorities. (See Chapter 10, *Observing, Recording, and Reporting on Children's Development*.) Next, the caregiver observes the child and identifies the daily routines that the child finds most enjoyable or engaging. A routine that is pleasant and successfully accomplished gives a child confidence and self-esteem. For example, if Barbara (the caregiver) observes that Julia loves to roll and unroll her mat for naptime, she can ask Julia to help her unroll some of the other children's mats.

## Levels of Support

After the caregiver selects the individualized goal(s) or skill(s) appropriate to a child, such as learning to put on her jacket, she decides what type of support is needed to guide the child in acquiring this skill. The level of support can be viewed on a continuum. A low level of support would be to lay the jacket on the floor for the child to slip over and put on. A high level of support would be to hold the jacket for the child, guiding each arm into the sleeve.

Whenever possible, the low-level support strategies should be tried first. If it is a new skill or behavior, the child may need more intensive support. However, as a child becomes used to the routine, a simple pause or expectant look may eventually be sufficient.

If the infant or toddler will never be able to perform the skill or behavior independently due to disabilities, then the caregiver should provide the support necessary to ensure that the child can participate in the routine or activity.

## Children With Special Needs

Caregivers have to plan quite carefully for infants and toddlers with special needs. Their routines, activities, and interactions often call for thoughtful, intensive planning. The methodical caregiver will do the following:

- Identify goals and skills appropriate for the child.
- Select opportunities within each routine to practice the skills.
- Determine what and how much support is necessary for this child's optimal development.

The caregiver supports the child's growth and development by helping and guiding the child through the routine or activity. It is important for the caregiver to know what and how much support to give. The caregiver may use other children as models to teach a toddler how to use his spoon correctly or pick up blocks and toys. Special chairs or other equipment, eating utensils, and toys may be needed to support the child's growth toward independence.

# Sample Daily Curriculum Chart

| <u>Young Infants</u> | <u>Mobile Infants</u> | <u>Toddlers</u> |
|---|---|---|
| <u>Note:</u><br>While the following learning opportunities are presented as a part of a daily "curriculum" chart, clearly a young infant's day should be individualized. It cannot and should not be scheduled.<br><br>• Arrival - greetings<br>• Play (solo, watching others)<br>• Lap times (singing, looking at a book, etc.)<br>• Diapering<br>• Meals<br>• Snacks<br>• Bottles<br>• Transition to rest/sleep<br>• Wake-up times<br>• Outdoor time<br>• Departure | <u>7:00-9:00</u><br>Arrival - Greetings<br>Diapering<br>Breakfast<br>Play - Private or Peer<br>(Rest as needed)<br><br><u>9:00-10:00</u><br>Music, stories, interactive games as desired<br>Large motor activities<br>Clean-up/Transition<br><br><u>10:00-11:30</u><br>Activity time: blocks, books, push/pull toys<br>Indoor or outdoor activities<br>(Feeding, diapering, toileting as needed)<br><br><u>11:30-12:00</u><br>Transition to Lunch: Lunch, diapering, handwashing<br><br><u>12:00-2:00</u><br>Naptime<br><br><u>2:00-3:00</u><br>Wake-up - Greetings<br>Diapering/Toileting<br>Snack<br>Play - Private or Peer<br><br><u>3:00-4:00</u><br>Activity Time<br><br><u>4:00-6:00</u><br>Music, stories, interactive games<br>Clean up/Transition<br>(Diapering/Toileting as needed)<br>Departure | <u>7:00-9:00</u><br>Arrival - Greetings<br>Diapering/Toileting<br>Breakfast<br>Play - Private or Peer<br><br><u>9:00-10:00</u><br>Table top activities<br>Group time - music and movement<br>Clean-up/Transition<br><br><u>10:00-11:30</u><br>Center/Activity time: art, dramatic play, blocks, story corner, music (Toileting as needed)<br><br><u>11:30-12:00</u><br>Transition to Lunch: Lunch, toileting, handwashing<br><br><u>12:00-2:00</u><br>Naptime<br><br><u>2:00-3:00</u><br>Wake-up - Greetings<br>Diapering/Toileting<br>Snack<br>Play - Private or Peer<br><br><u>3:00-4:00</u><br>Activity Time<br><br><u>4:00-6:00</u><br>Table top activities<br>Group time - music and movement<br>Clean up/Transition<br>Diapering/Toileting<br>Departure |

## Sample Weekly Developmental Matrix - Toddlers

| Date | Monday | Tuesday | Wednesday | Thursday | Friday |
|---|---|---|---|---|---|
| **Arrival** | Says "hello" Puts bag in cubby | Says "hello" Puts bag in cubby | Says "hello" Puts bag in cubby | Says "hello" Puts bag in cubby | Says "hello" Puts bag in cubby |
| **Feeding** | Vocalizes needs Cleans up | Passes food Cleans up | Labels food and drink Cleans up | Labels food and drink Cleans up | Labels food and drink Cleans up |
| **Play** | Takes turns with 1-2 peers Answers questions | Pretend play Uses 3-word sentences | Climbs on low objects Throws and catches large ball | Pretend play Indicates needs | Pretend play Indicates needs |
| **Diapering/ Toileting** | Pulls pants down Washes hands | Pulls pants down Washes hands | Identifies body parts Washes hands | Identifies body parts Washes hands | Pulls pants down Attempts to pull pants up |
| **Lunch** | Eats with a spoon | Labels food items Cleans up | Responds to requests Follows lunch routine | Responds to requests Follows lunch routine | Responds to requests Follows lunch routine |
| **Nap** | | | | | |
| **Snack** | Requests food Indicates when finished | Follows simple directions Cleans up | Sorts snack materials Cleans up | Sorts snack materials Cleans up | Sorts snack materials Cleans up |
| **Play** | Puts toys away Indicates protest Dress-up | Hide-and-seek games Plays chase | Builds with blocks Labels familiar toys and materials | Fills and dumps Plays kick ball Uses 3-word sentences | Fills and dumps Plays kick ball Uses 3-word sentences |
| **Departure** | Points to clothing Says "good-bye" | Expresses affection Pulls on outer garments | Says "good-bye" Sorts personal items | Says "good-bye" Sorts personal items | Says "good-bye" Sorts personal items |

## Sample Developmental Goals Chart

| Daily Routines | Young Infants | Mobile Infants | Toddlers |
|---|---|---|---|
| Arrival | * smiles<br>* reaches<br>* responds to voices<br>* coos/babbles | * waves "hello"<br>* vocalizes<br>* begins to take off outer clothes | * says "hello"<br>* walks carrying bag<br>* takes off outer clothes<br>* hangs up bag in cubby |
| Feeding | * cries/fusses to indicate hunger<br>* makes eye contact<br>* smiles, vocalizes<br>* turns toward voices and sounds<br>* reaches/holds a bottle | * points/gestures<br>* holds a bottle or cup<br>* eats crackers, finger foods<br>* begins to use utensils to eat | * communicates hunger verbally<br>* climbs into chair<br>* eats independently<br>* uses thumb & forefinger to pick up small objects<br>* indicates "more"<br>* labels food items<br>* washes & dries hands |
| Diapering/Toileting | * cries/fusses to indicate discomfort<br>* makes eye contact<br>* smiles, vocalizes<br>* imitates sounds<br>* may roll over or kick legs<br>* grasps objects | * cries/fusses to indicate discomfort<br>* points/gestures to indicate need<br>* helps by holding bottom up and putting feet into pants legs<br>* responds to directions | * may verbalize need to be changed or to go to the bathroom<br>* initiates toileting<br>* unfastens clothing<br>* stays dry longer<br>* washes and dries hands<br>* acknowledges going to the bathroom |
| Dressing | * coos/babbles<br>* plays "peek-a-boo"<br>* begins to bend arms and legs to cooperate<br>* looks at self in mirror<br>* looks for dropped objects | * initiates own dressing games<br>* removes small clothing items<br>* assists in putting on clothes and moving arms and legs | * dresses in simple, large clothes<br>* names clothing, common objects<br>* opinionated on fabrics, colors, items<br>* removes clothing with little or no assistance<br>* shows body parts<br>* follows two simple directions |

| Daily Routines | Young Infants | Mobile Infants | Toddlers |
|---|---|---|---|
| Napping/Sleeping | * cries/fusses when tired or alert<br>* rolls over<br>* recognizes familiar faces and objects upon waking<br>* anticipates returns | * going-to-sleep ritual lengthens<br>* cries/fusses when tired<br>* points/gestures to crib or sleep area | * points/gestures when tired<br>* verbalizes desire or need to sleep<br>* may resist sleep<br>* helps with tasks (puts blankets away) |
| Private Play | *observes own hands and feet<br>* reaches for and grasps toys<br>* sits with support<br>* transfers toys from hand to hand<br>* sucks hands and fingers | * smiles at or plays with self in mirror<br>* gets into sitting<br>* explores environment, objects<br>* crawls, cruises, walks with support<br>* scribbles<br>* turns pages of book<br>* seeks out preferred toys | * plays pretend games<br>* explores surroundings<br>* plays alone<br>* shows affection to dolls, people<br>* colors, paints<br>* jumps<br>* takes things apart and puts them together<br>* names pictures in book |
| Peer Play | * coos/babbles<br>* shows dislike when familiar toy is removed<br>* makes eye contact | * explores objects with others<br>* shows interest in peers<br>* initiates social games | * listens to stories, rhymes, music<br>* completes simple puzzles<br>* plays pretend games, role plays<br>* throws ball with aim |
| Departure | * may greet parent happily or be matter-of-fact<br>* smiles back at adults<br>* recognizes parent<br>* controls head when carried | * may be absorbed in activity and resist leaving<br>* may resent parent for leaving and ignore or resist<br>* uses words like mama and bye-bye<br>* waves, vocalizes | * may protest leaving<br>* can pick up and put away toys after activity<br>* answers simple questions<br>* uses personal pronouns |

# CHAPTER 10

# OBSERVING, RECORDING, AND REPORTING ON CHILDREN'S DEVELOPMENT

# 10. OBSERVING, RECORDING, AND REPORTING ON CHILDREN'S DEVELOPMENT

Systematic observation is fundamental to a quality child care program. The overarching purpose of observation is to gather information that can be shared with parents and other caregivers and used to plan activities and routines that best meet the individual needs of the infants and toddlers in the program. This chapter explains why we observe, what we observe, how to observe, when to observe, various recording methods, and how to use observation information that is collected.

## Why We Observe

How do teachers and caregivers know if their program's approach and its activities are meeting the children's cognitive, social, emotional, physical and language needs? How can they share information with parents in a way that accurately describes how the children are spending their time? How do teachers document a concern about a particular child's behavior? How can teachers work on improving their performance? How do they assure themselves that they are giving equal time and attention to all of the children assigned to them? How and when do they report their observations to other teachers or parents?

Observation techniques help teachers and caregivers answer these questions objectively. Their observations, which focus both on children and the caregiving environment, have several specific purposes:

- To be aware of each child's development
- To understand each child's temperament
- To understand how the children interact as a group and how individuals within the group react to each other
- To evaluate whether and how teachers and the physical surroundings respond to the needs of each child

## Observation

Observation is the process of watching an infant or toddler, usually without interfering in the activity. As she observes a child's response to daily routines and activities, the caregiver is gathering information about the child's skill levels, temperament, preferences, and overall development.

## Recording

Recording is the process of documenting the information gathered through observation. Through systematic recording the caregiver can compare what she sees now with what she saw in previous recorded observations. Memories fade and blur over time. Written records make accurate comparisons possible over extended periods.

## Reporting

Reporting is the process of sharing observations with parents and other caregivers. Sharing information makes it more likely that everyone involved will respond to the child in a consistent manner. If the observer has a specific concern about a child, it should be part of the written record, to be used as a source of information for caregivers, parents, and any outside specialists the parents consult.

## *What We Observe*

### Developmental Progress

Caregivers need to know the social, physical, cognitive, and emotional characteristics of each child so they can plan and respond in ways that promote the development of the whole child. For a child who is developing typically, this knowledge helps caregivers focus on emerging skills, interests, and preferences, so that they can promote interactions and activities that support the child's natural developmental cycles.

Careful observation also alerts caregivers to a child who is developing atypically or more slowly than others. Parents and caregivers who see the child every day are the "first alert system" about developmental progress. Caregivers who know what typical infant and toddler development looks like, and how broad the variations in that development

120

can be, are especially well suited to identify children not developing typically. As they observe infants' and toddlers' responses to daily activities and routines and interview parents, caregivers use systematic observation and recording methods. One such method is a developmental checklist which caregivers can use to systematically organize their observations. A checklist helps caregivers identify *patterns* of behavior that provide important information that help the caregiver and parents understand a child. These patterns often alert caregivers to subtle clues that a particular infant or toddler may have special needs. For example, it is obvious to parents and caregivers that something is wrong if a child cannot walk by age two but, without attentive, systematic caregiver observation, other less obvious problems are likely to be missed. Staff should discuss any suspected developmental delay or disability with the child's parents and help parents get any necessary referrals for a full developmental evaluation. Caregivers should also devise program strategies for additional support and stimulation that will benefit the child.

Each caregiver should also observe the health and physical development of her assigned children periodically. All children should have regular vision and hearing examinations. Depending on local regulations, this can be done by a visiting health professional or the center's usual physician. (See Appendix A, *Developmental Milestones of Children from Birth to Age 3*.)

## Temperament

Children's temperaments influence what they do, what and how they learn, how they feel about themselves and others, and how they react and interact. As caregivers observe infants and toddlers, they detect patterns in the ways that individual children typically react to situations. Caregivers use that information to plan routines, activities, and inter-actions adapted to each child's unique temperament. For example, a caregiver will develop strategies to help a shy child relate to the group without exposing him to uncomfortable situations.

Caregivers observe and record children's responses to the daily routines of eating, toileting, sleeping, arriving, and departing. By observing a child's typical responses to daily activities, caregivers understand how the child mobilizes his various developmental skills to perform a task. (See Chapter 9 for additional information about daily routines.)

## Interactions With Other Children

In addition to understanding each child's individual characteristics, caregivers must also understand the dynamics of the group: How do the children react and interact with each other? Caregivers observe and record who plays with whom, which children choose which activities, and which materials and toys are favored This kind of analysis may show that one rather passive child is ignored most of the time, or that another child regularly monopolizes a favorite doll that others would like to play with.

## Impact of the Physical Environment and of Caregivers on Children

Children are affected by their environment: the space itself, the things in it, and their caregivers. The observer will want to know whether the environment responds to or interferes with a child's growth and development. A caregiver will want to know how a child interacts with her, with other staff/team members, and with family members. Team members can take turns observing each other objectively and carefully, and recording and sharing their observations.

## Caregiver and Child Interactions

Caregivers should be alert to behaviors that elicit a positive response from a child. One infant may enjoy a soothing song when her diaper is being changed, while another prefers a game of "Peek-a-Boo". Caregivers should also be aware of behavior that may interfere with a child's development: for example, a caregiver who speaks rapidly or mumbles cannot be understood by a child who is just beginning to develop language skills.

## Family and Cultural Influences

In keeping with the Step by Step philosophy, caregivers are careful to understand and respect the culture of each child's family. (See Chapters 1 and 11 for a broader discussion.) Therefore, it is important that team members and their supervisors monitor each other as they respond to children of different backgrounds, to ensure that no child or group of children receive anything less than the full support and encouragement that they deserve.

## Schedule

Children of different ages and temperaments need different schedules. Through observation, caregivers identify the best time for quiet activities, group play, rest time, and private play. A caregiver can observe whether a particular child needs more frequent feedings, an earlier rest time, or more time for private play, and adjust that child's schedule accordingly.

## Physical Environment

Careful observation will show whether the environment meets the varied needs of infants and toddlers. Caregivers should ask whether the physical surroundings are clean, pleasant, comfortable, and suitable for a variety of activities. Is there enough space for all the activities that occur on a typical day? If the physical environment has shortcomings, it should be modified so that it will serve the best interests of the children and their caregivers.

## Children With Special Needs

Careful observations can draw caregivers' attention to subtle, previously unnoticed environmental features that impede children with special needs. Similarly, careful observation can show caregivers (1) how the environment should be modified to help a child who is has a physical disability, or (2) how teachers might respond to stimulate a child who is developmentally delayed. Is certain equipment inaccessible to a child? Does he always avoid it for some reason which could be easily accommodated?

Toddlers can learn very early to respect and help others. Experienced teachers have found that close observation of a group's dynamics often reveals that children are helping, or want to help, a child with special needs.

## *How We Observe*

Recorded observations describe what a child did in a particular situation. They should be purposeful, objective, and descriptive of behavior. The information recorded grows out of the purpose of the observation. In other words, the observer does not begin until she has decided what questions she wants answered by the observation.

## *When We Observe*

Obviously, it is impossible to be a warm, responsive teacher and, at the same time, step back to systematically observe and record what is happening. Caregivers and their supervisor or director should build observation times into the schedule, so that every teacher has regular and frequent opportunities to observe. Other staff can take turns sharing the added caregiving responsibilities.

In addition to scheduled, somewhat formal observation, caregivers also find self-observation extremely valuable. Although informal and less objective than being observed by someone else, self-observation keeps the caregiver alert to her own attitudes, actions, and behaviors on an ongoing basis.

### During Play

A child at play is her most active and self-directed self. Play provides an excellent opportunity to observe since, by definition, the activities are not structured or scheduled by adults. What is she most interested in playing with? Does she persist with one activity for a long time, or does she get frustrated or lose attention early and move on to another toy? Does she like to play with another child or prefer to play alone?

### During Daily Routines

Routines are also good settings for gathering information about children and their environment. How does an infant react to being dressed? Is she fearful at naptime? Does a caregiver show patience as a toddler attempts to wash her hands? Does a parent take time to say good-bye to a child in the morning, or does she leave abruptly? Does the time of day seem to affect a child's behavior? Is her behavior predictable from one routine to another? How does a child typically react to routines? Is she restless, energetic, listless, compliant? Please read the following examples.

### Arrival and Departure
(The method used is formal observation by another caregiver.)

As a mother and her toddler arrive, the observer asks: Does the child make eye contact with the teacher as he meets her in the morning? With the parent at the end of the day? Does he crawl or walk toward the teacher in the morning? Toward the parent at day's end? Does he seem to ignore the parent? How does he react to the caregiver? If he is distressed, is he able to comfort himself? Does the teacher's attention comfort him?

### Feeding
(This caregiver uses an informal self-observation method.)

> *Joshua (7 months old) sits in Karen's lap while enjoying his bottle. He sucks vigorously for several minutes, then turns his head to look up at Karen. She smiles at him and softly says, "Mmm, that's good, isn't it, Joshua? Do you want some more?" She places the bottle next to his mouth and he turns and resumes eating. He stops again and begins to flail his arms and arch his back. Karen slightly adjusts his position on her lap and he begins eating again.*

Karen has learned many things while observing and feeding Joshua. She has learned how he communicates his desire for more food, for a rest from eating, for an adjustment of his body in her arms. Over time she has learned how much he typically eats during his morning feeding, and notices if he eats significantly more or less on any given day. She will be able to give his parents a detailed account of his day and the way he responds to eating.

# Recording Observation Information

There are many ways to record observations. Some of the most useful are anecdotal records, narrative or diary records, caregiver observation checklists, frequency counts and time samples, and media tools like photographs, audiotapes, and videotapes.

## Anecdotal Records

These are brief written "snapshots" that describe specific actions and events. They tell a "picture in words" at a particular moment. They are useful for child assessment and individualized planning. It is essential that anecdotal records be objective. Objective observations are factual and descriptive:

> *Maria walks across the room carrying several plastic shapes in her hands. She offers one of the shapes to Sophie, her caregiver, and says, "Ga, ba, ba, da?" Sophie smiles and says, "Thank you, Maria."*

In contrast, subjective observations include labels, judgments, or information recorded out of context. Subjective observations are not useful for assessment or planning, because interpretations of actions or behaviors interfere with the observation itself. This is a subjective observation:

> *Jonathan is constantly taking Michael's truck. He is a mean child.*

This statement does not give objective information. We do not know what the observer means by "constantly." It is the observer's opinion that Jonathan is "mean." "Mean" is a label. It does not convey information that helps someone else understand Jonathan's development. It is an adult's interpretation and should not be used.

The observer should ask these questions:

- What happened immediately before the activity or behavior?
  - √ What prompted the child to do this activity or behavior?
  - √ Did the teacher initiate the activity?
  - √ Did the child notice others and copy them?
- What is the physical setting?
  - √ What was the surrounding physical environment?
  - √ Who are the significant people nearby?
  - √ What are they doing?
- What is the child's reaction? What does the child do?
- What does the child do immediately after the activity or behavior?

Anecdotal records also can include direct quotations of what someone said, as well as *objective* descriptions of the quality of the behavior:

> *Nina jumped six inches off the ground, remarkably high for a child her age.*

## Narratives or Diary Records

Daily notes, stories, or short descriptions of group and individual activities recorded at the end of the day can be useful additions to the child's Care Log. (Care Logs are described later in this chapter.) While narratives or diary records tend to be more subjective than anecdotal observations, they can record an impression or mood, identify successes or failures of the day's events, and offer ongoing insights to a child's behaviors. For example:

*Mary seemed to be afraid of the peek-a-boo game we played while diapering. She cried when I covered my face. We stopped the game and did not try it again.*

*Sliding down the little slide was fun for all three of the children. Everyone shouted with excitement. We needed to be careful not to go too fast for Abigail, who was youngest. It was a good chance to practice climbing steps, as well as sliding.*

## Caregiver Observation Checklists

A developmental checklist itemizes a child's observable and measurable behaviors, usually in a developmental sequence. It is used to collect information on a child's developmental level. Other observational checklists guide caregivers as they observe children's interests, learning styles, or temperament. (A sample *Temperament Observation Form* is offered at the end of this chapter.)

## Frequency Counts and Time Samples

Observers use these techniques to measure the number of times a behavior occurs and its duration. By tracking this information over time, the observer can identify a pattern of behavior (when it occurs, how often, and with whom). The observer can then identify patterns of behavior that may be detrimental to a child's healthy growth or her relationships with other children. The following is an example of a frequency count:

*Tanya pulled on her hair five times during a ten-minutes story time, three times during lunch, and four times before falling asleep.*

The following are examples of time sample observations:

*Cassia cried for ten minutes after her mother left the center. That was five minutes less than yesterday.*

*Alex played with the stack of cups for twenty minutes without stopping.*

127

## Observation Media

Some of the best (but not essential) ways to capture complex interactions of young children as they play and interact with each other and the caregiver are to use videotape, audiotape, or photographs. Each can be used to document individual development and group interactions. However, videotape is especially helpful when analyzing group dynamics or caregiver behavior.

# *Organizing Observation Information*

Observation records for each child can be organized in a variety of ways:

## Care Log

A *Care Log* is a permanent record of a child's progress, documented in a series of observation forms and checklists, organized in a loose-leaf notebook or file for safekeeping. The Log is a detailed, day-to-day record of a child's development, health, daily routines, and activities. Caregivers and parents jointly develop and maintain *Care Logs*, which may include parent observations. (See the sample *Care Log* at the end of this chapter.)

In the *Care Log* parents may report an event that happened at home, ask questions, or comment on their child's response to a situation. Caregivers put their written responses to parents' notes in the *Care Log*, or invite parents to meet and discuss their concerns. *Care Logs are always kept in a private and secure place to protect families' privacy.* (See Chapter 11, *Families and Caregivers Together*, for an extended discussion of communication and confidentiality between parents and caregivers.)

## Routines and Activities

Since the simple routines of eating, sleeping, and toileting take up so much time in the lives of infants and toddlers, caregivers and parents must keep each other informed about these routines. Caregivers can record the events of the day and any unusual response to those events. Parents can do the same. (Sample forms are included at the end of Chapter 11, *Families and Caregivers Together*.)

## Special Information

The *Care Log* is also used to record injuries, unusual events, or behavior that is atypical for that child. For example, if an infant is usually active, but has been quiet and withdrawn for several days, caregivers will note that unusual behavior and, in consultation with parents, try to determine its cause. Is he becoming ill? Has his mother been away?

## *How to Use Observation Information*

The purpose of observation and recording is to gather information that can be shared with families and other caregivers and used to improve the overall program.

### Sharing Information With Families

The *Care Log* records a child's activities, response patterns, and developmental progress. As the caregiver and family use the *Care Log* to share and exchange information, the Log has two functions:

- **Communication** As parents and caregivers contribute to the Log, their patterns of communication are strengthened.
- **Connection** The Log connects parents and teachers to each other as they work together in the best interests of the child.

*Care Log* entries need not be very lengthy or formal. However, they should be constant and ongoing, maintaining a record not only from day to day but also from month to month.

### Adapting the Environment

A primary purpose of observation is to evaluate how caregivers and the environment respond to the needs of each child. The program staff asks questions like these:

- Does the environment support and reflect the Step by Step Program's philosophy and goals?
- Does the environment encourage children to explore? to initiate? to create?
- Does each aspect of the environment—the physical surroundings, emotional climate, daily routines, daily activities, and the attitudes and behaviors of teachers—help to individualize learning experiences for each child?
- Does each aspect of the environment encourage children to make choices?

If the answer to any of these is no, the team adjusts, adapts, or modifies whatever is not working. If, for example, the teachers observe that many of the toddlers are irritable and cranky at a particular time of day, they modify the daily schedule, making snack time 30 minutes earlier.

## *Conclusion*

Observation, recording, and reporting are basic to a child-centered program. This chapter has summarized the various ways in which these processes can improve the quality of care, help staff to focus on the needs of particular children, and share their observations with families.

## TEMPERAMENT OBSERVATION FORM

| Temperament Traits | Child Observations |
| --- | --- |
| **1. <u>Activity Level</u>**<br>How active or restless is the child? Does the child lie fairly still or does the child repeatedly kick while sleeping and squirm frequently while diapering? Is the toddler always running, climbing, jumping? Does he spend a lot of time observing and playing quietly? | |
| **2. <u>Regularity</u>**<br>How predictable is the child in her patterns of sleep, appetite, bowel habits? | |
| **3. <u>Approach-Withdrawal</u>**<br>What is the child's usual response to new people, places, foods, clothes? | |
| **4. <u>Adaptability</u>**<br>How does the child deal with transition and change? | |
| **5. <u>Sensory Threshold</u>**<br>How does the child react to sensory stimuli: noise, bright lights, colors, smells, pain, tastes, the texture and feel of clothes? Is the child easily overstimulated? | |
| **6. <u>Intensity of Reaction</u>**<br>How loud is the child generally, whether happy or unhappy? | |
| **7. <u>Mood</u>**<br>What is the child's basic disposition? Is the child usually smiling/carefree or more serious? | |
| **8. <u>Distractibility</u>**<br>How easily is the child distracted? What does the child pay attention to? | |
| **9. <u>Persistence</u>**<br>Once involved with something does the child stay with it for a long time? How determined is she when she wants something? | |

# CARE LOG

DAILY LOG

Date:

Child:

Parent Observation:

_____

_____

_____

_____

_____

_____

Parent Signature:

Caregiver Comment:

_____

_____

_____

_____

_____

_____

Caregiver Signature:

# CHAPTER 11

# FAMILIES AND CAREGIVERS TOGETHER SUPPORTING INFANTS AND TODDLERS

# 11. FAMILIES AND CAREGIVERS TOGETHER SUPPORTING INFANTS AND TODDLERS

The decision to place an infant or toddler in an early childhood program is often a very emotional one for families. Parents may have conflicting emotions about the decision, questions about the care their child will receive, concerns about the teachers' responsiveness, and questions about the safety of the environment. They may even worry about their child's growing attachment to another adult. All these factors will influence how the family feels about enrolling their precious child in a child care program. It is important for the staff to begin to build partnerships with families from the day of enrollment.

Families are infants' first and primary teachers. Therefore, staff must work together with families to support their routines, schedules, culture, and concerns. At the same time, staff must remember that, like their infants, the families are learning too. This is a new and unique member of the family and they are learning about the child's characteristics, temperament, style, likes, and dislikes. The infant and toddler program builds upon this primary relationship between child and family by providing ongoing opportunities for families to feel connected with the program and to view it as a valuable resource.

The program team should provide family members with many different opportunities to be involved in the program. They should communicate with each family daily, sharing news of the child's day, and informing families of planned activities and meetings. They should get to know the infants and families through home visits, scheduled at times convenient to the family. They should encourage families to visit the classroom at any time, to breast- or bottle- feed their babies, play with their toddlers, or talk with the staff. The team should be alert to opportunities for exchanging information. Some families may want to be deeply involved; others may not. The amount and frequency of communication, beyond the basic essentials, should depend upon a family's needs and preferences.

This chapter covers five main topics: getting to know families, communicating with families, communication strategies, involving families, and confidentiality.

## Getting to Know Families

Give families specific information when they enroll their child. Invite them to visit the center for a tour and introduction to other staff members. This visit will establish the connection for continued partnership. When explaining the program, use inclusive phrases like "our program" or "we will work together" or "as a team we will. . . " This communicates to the family that you want to work with them.

Team members need to understand families' concerns, reminding them that no one can take their place and that the team is there to support them. Reassure families that you will support their values and culture. They also need to know they are welcome to visit the program at any time.

When families first visit, take time to show them where their child will spend his day, tell them about the safety, health, and sanitary procedures, and explain the policies and procedures regarding feeding, toilet training, and sleeping. Reassure them that the team, particularly the primary caregiver, will give them a daily report on their child's activities. Show them the kitchen, the diapering area, the bathrooms, and the sleeping, feeding, and play areas. Give a tour of the outdoor area and explain its safety features. Show them the Family Room. Explain parent meetings, newsletters, and the parents' bulletin board. Let them know that classroom helpers are always needed and welcome. As you create an atmosphere of honesty and openness, families will feel more comfortable asking questions and expressing their concerns.

Give each family a *Parent Handbook* that includes basic information about the program, including the Step by Step philosophy, policies, procedures, the Family Room, lending library, and parent meetings. One section of the *Handbook* should discuss the very important role of families and should state what is expected of parents. Families who are already enrolled in the program can be very helpful in developing the *Handbook* and keeping it up to date.

## Involving Families

From the very first time the families are asked if they want to participate in the program, they should get the message that you want them to be involved in as many ways as possible. It may be a new idea for them and they may not welcome it at first. Involving families in a meaningful way takes time, planning, and knowledge about their interests and other commitments.

Use a *Family Interest Survey* to find out whether and how a family wants to participate. Present this survey form at one of the first parent meetings and explain its purpose so families do not feel intimidated by it. (A sample letter and a *Family Interest Survey* are available at the end of this chapter.)

You will discover other needs, interests, and talents of families throughout the year as trust increases and relationships grow stronger.

## *Communicating With Families*

Communicating with families about their children is a fundamental part of the teaching team's responsibilities. Since infants are totally dependent on caregivers to meet their basic needs, it is essential for teachers and parents to communicate daily about the infant's well-being, health status and comfort level, as well as her eating, toileting, sleeping, and playing routines. Toddlers, although more independent than infants, still rely on the adults in their lives to provide for their basic needs: physical and emotional health and developmental stimulation. Again, daily communication is crucial. All families love and care about their children and want them to be healthy, secure, successful, and happy. The Infant and Toddler Program is the child's first experience away from home, and family members will want to know about the child's progress. The teaching team will want to discuss the child's home schedule, food preferences, toileting methods, health issues, and any areas of concern with families, so routines and preferences are as consistent as possible. (This is the time for parents to fill out the *Child Information Sheet*, and *What You Should Know About Me* located at the end of this chapter, and the *Child Health Information Questionnaire* shown at the end of Chapter 12, *Ensuring a Healthy Environment*.)

## Expectations

Many programs have discovered there may be differences between the expectations or goals of the caregiving team and those of the family. It is important to discuss the philosophy of the program with families during enrollment, the first home visit, and throughout the year. If parents or caregivers are not aware of the differences, misunderstandings or faulty communication will result. Ask families how they expect the program to benefit their children and what they think is most important for their children's care and learning.

## Communication Techniques

Some parents may have had negative experiences during their own schooling and may feel uncomfortable or intimidated by schools and teachers. Others may have been taught that teachers "know what's best" and should not be questioned. Teachers may also have had negative experiences: perhaps parents have told them how to teach, or have disregarded their well-meaning advice on issues such as toileting, feeding, and behavior. Because these attitudes or feelings can interfere with good communication, it is especially important to take the time and effort to communicate.

> ***Active Listening*** Active listening techniques require listening very carefully and respectfully to parents' messages. It means looking into a parent's eyes, being encouraging, nodding, and, if you are not sure what the parent meant, repeating what you think was said for clarification.

***Unspoken Communication (Body Language)***  At times, family members are uncomfortable directly discussing an issue they feel strongly about.  Being able to understand unspoken communication (body language) may alert you that something is bothering the parent.  For example, if you notice that a mother becomes very tense when discussing her child's eating habits, you should take special care to listen and follow up with gentle questions.

***Open-Ended Questions***  Unlike questions that call for yes or no answers, open-ended questions offer opportunities for family members to tell you about their children.  When you ask, "What is Natalie's day like at home?" "Please tell us about her sleeping and eating routines." or "What are Matthew's favorite toys?" parents are more likely to share information than if you ask, "Does Natalie nap in the afternoon?"

***Honest and Direct Information***  Sharing honest and direct information with family members helps build trust over time.  Parents begin to believe that the caregiver will tell them the truth about their child, even if the information is hard for them to hear.  For example, a teacher who suspects that a child has a hearing loss will share this information with the parents and refer them to a hearing specialist.

## Communicating About Difficult Issues

Some issues require not only a great deal of sensitivity but also a good understanding of one's own emotions and reactions to situations.

***Separation***  Saying good-bye is hard for young children and family members.  Acknowledging this difficulty is the first step in establishing the trust necessary to smooth the separation process.  Young infants who are establishing their own individual routines for sleeping, feeding, moving, and interacting with their environment need a comfortable crib, a familiar toy, and most important, someone who understands their cues for comforting, nurturing, feeding, sleeping, and active times.  Mobile infants have a hard time leaving their parents and need a routine that helps them feel safe and secure.  Reassure parents that "stranger anxiety" is a typical developmental milestone that usually occurs around nine months.  Caregivers and parents should work together to develop comfortable ways to help infants leave their parents with as little stress as possible.  For example, they might join their child in playing with a toy, not leaving until the child is happily engrossed.

Toddlers are better able to separate when they know what to expect.  Their daily schedule should be orderly and consistent.  Sometimes it helps if the child brings something from home, like a favorite blanket, stuffed animal, or other familiar toy, to ease the transition.  The teacher can also help the child ease into the classroom by offering a favorite activity and reassuring the child that her parents will return at a certain time. Having a picture of the family that the child can look at sometimes eases the separation.

In all cases, infants and toddlers need one caring adult to greet them, to help them say good-bye to their parents—one who knows them well enough to make the transition from home to school a safe, positive experience. Do not forget that parents may also experience sadness, anxiety, and guilt when they leave their child. Let them know that you understand their feelings and assure them that you will take very good care of their baby. At the same time, they should be comfortable knowing that you are not in competition for their child's affection.

***Cultural Preferences*** Families from diverse cultures have diverse child-rearing traditions and beliefs. It is important for the caregiving team to learn about the cultural backgrounds of the infants and toddlers in the program. The best way to gain cultural information is by asking parents to share information with you. Ask about food preferences, discipline expectations, health practices, religious and cultural holidays, and celebrations. Beware of stereotypes. Do not assume that all members of a particular ethnic or religious group are alike or share the same characteristics. Each family is unique and has its own traditions.

Invite family members into the classroom to sing a special song, share a folk-tale, prepare a customary food, or explain a holiday. When the caregiver recognizes and celebrates the diversity of the children, it shows respect for them and an interest in knowing all aspects of their lives.

A family may speak a language other than the majority language used in the classrooms. Learn some of the family's language and teach simple words and phrases like "hello," "good-bye," "thank you," "how are you?" and "I am sorry " to a small group of toddlers. Or, invite a parent to teach these phrases. The toddlers will enjoy the novelty and they will be learning to communicate in a world of many languages. Let the classroom reflect the cultures of the children through traditional toys, music, books, and pictures.

All classrooms will have children whose parents have a variety of parenting styles. Cultural differences occasionally lead to misunderstanding and conflict between home and school. For this reason, it is important to convey the program's child-rearing philosophy and practices *before* the parents enroll their child. If the parents are uncomfortable with the program's approaches, they may choose to send their child to another program. If a family's traditional approach to child-rearing is not acceptable to the program, carefully describe the differences without making the parents feel that they are bad parents.

Common areas of conflict include feeding, toileting, sleeping and discipline practices. When she eats at home a toddler is expected to finish everything on her plate, while at school the rule is that she has to taste everything but does not have to finish something she dislikes. At school a toddler is told, "No, Thomas, Kathy is playing with that now," when he grabs Kathy's toy, he is redirected to another activity. At home a parent might gently hit Thomas on the hand to stop him from grabbing. Although consistency is important for children, they can learn that rules and expectations differ at home and at school. It is important to discuss these differences openly and clearly with families, and try to understand their point of view. Whenever possible, without violating the philosophy of the program, try to accommodate parental choice.

***Coping With Jealousy*** Parents are sometimes fearful of losing their child's love, fearful that their child will prefer his caregiver. They may wish that they could be with their infant or toddler throughout the day. They may feel jealous of the attachment between caregiver and child. To help parents cope with these feelings, the caregiver can:

- Encourage the parent to visit the classroom more often
- Post pictures of the family on the crib or walls
- Ask for a favorite toy or blanket from home
- Encourage the toddler to draw a special picture for a parent
- Communicate regularly

## Communicating About Routines

Routines such as feeding, toileting, and sleeping are among the most important activities in the infant and toddler classroom. Chapters 8 and 9 discussed the use of various routines for developmental purposes. Here we will discuss issues that may cause tension between parents and staff and present strategies for resolving conflicts that arise.

*Feeding* Caregivers and parents should work together to solve problems that may arise over issues such as:

- When to give up a bottle
- How to encourage children to eat a variety of foods
- "Rules" for how much or how little food is acceptable for the child to eat
- How to avoid "power struggles" over food
- What foods are recommended for healthy and nutritious snacks

Caregivers must keep careful records on each child's preferred foods, feeding schedules, and any food allergies. Keep parents informed about any digestive upset, new foods, and their infant's general attitudes toward food. Post the weekly meal and snack schedule and give a copy to each family. Daily communication about feeding is essential.

*Toileting* Understandably, parents are upset when they arrive at the center to find their infant with soaked diapers or an unexplained diaper rash. A baby cannot be changed the very instant a diaper is soiled, but time should be scheduled for frequent changes during the day. Explain or demonstrate your diapering routine; it reassures parents and can give them ideas for easy diapering at home.

Toilet training is a complex interplay between readiness, behavioral change, and predictable routines. (Chapter 12, *Ensuring a Healthy Environment*, discusses healthy toileting practices and Chapter 9 discussed using diapering and toileting as learning experiences.) Caregivers must elicit the parents' perspectives on toilet training before starting to toilet train a child. Discuss the program's approach to toilet training. Explain developmental readiness and how your toileting routines are organized. Problems can occur when parents and teachers have different expectations about toilet training. Some parents want their child toilet trained at a very young age, and expect the teachers to avoid "accidents" by "catching" the child and putting her on the toilet. Others prefer to wait until their children have more conscious control over this function. It is important for staff and parents to discuss their different perspectives on this subject. Ideally, when parents learn about developmental readiness, they will be willing to wait. However, the area of toilet training varies enormously by culture, and caregivers should respect each family's point of view.

***Sleeping*** Infants vary greatly in their need for sleep and rest. Young infants should be allowed to follow what is natural for them in sleeping and being awake. Caregivers will quickly learn an infant's sleep patterns. It is appropriate for toddlers to have scheduled rest periods each day, but even then some children will fall asleep immediately, while others may play quietly for a long time before falling asleep.

Ask parents about their child's sleep patterns: How do they know when she is sleepy? What routines do they use when putting her to bed? How do they calm the baby? How does she awaken in the morning? Discuss the child's daytime sleep patterns with parents and ask for their help in dealing with any problems, such as excessive crying or colic. Together find a sleep routine that works. Some parents may ask to keep their toddler from taking a late nap because he cannot fall asleep easily at night, while others may encourage late napping because it gives them more waking time at home with their child. Try to accommodate parental choice. Each child has his own internal need for sleep. Finding a compromise is important. Perhaps a short afternoon nap from which the child is awakened by the teacher will suffice for the child who is having difficulty with going to bed, and a longer nap or a quiet rest time can be provided for the child with a later bedtime.

## Strategies for Communicating With Families

Because no one method of communication will work with all families, a variety of communication strategies is necessary to meet the diverse needs of the parents. Different strategies work best at different times.

### Drop-off and Pick-up Times

Busy schedules and work demands often leave families with very little extra time. Therefore, the natural informal occasions when team members and families can talk are valuable opportunities for establishing lines of communication between the home and school.

Experienced caregivers recommend talking briefly with families in the morning when parents deliver their children and again in the afternoon when they collect them. Afternoon is especially valuable because teachers can report on the day's routines and activities, tell families about their child's successes, and remind them of meetings or events. This informal time also allows families to talk with other parents, observe their child at play, ask questions, request a meeting, use classroom toys or games to interact with their own child, or read to a small group of children.

The classroom schedule must be flexible enough to allow for this valuable informal time with families. It should build in relaxed beginning and ending activities. To ensure that families don't just leave the children at the door, center policy should state clearly that families must bring children inside and help them get organized for the day. This is not, however, a time to discuss major concerns or problems of children, since they are present. Write a note to the parents and, if necessary, set up a special meeting for that purpose. Setting a time for a telephone conference may work best for busy families.

## Written Communication

A good way to communicate is to send a brief but informative note or other written information home with the child. A simple form can be filled out daily and given to the parents at the end of the day. (Sample sheets are *What I Did Today* and *Daily Information Sheet* located at the end of this chapter.) For infants, it is important to record their sleeping and activity periods, bowel movements, feeding times, what was eaten and how much, and other pertinent health or developmental information. For toddlers, notes can tell of an accomplishment, a new skill, new foods offered, progress with toilet training, behavior problems, or other noteworthy occurrences. If the caregiver is concerned about a child's health, inform his parents immediately and follow up with a written statement. If a child becomes sick during the day, call or send for the parents immediately and keep the child quiet, comforted, and away from other children until the parents arrive to take the child home or to a doctor. Tell parents of any falls, injuries, problems with other children, or unusual changes in mood or behavior at the end of the day or by telephone that evening, and follow-up with a written statement. It is recommended that the caregiver keep a copy in the child's Care Log also.

Families appreciate caregivers who keep them informed. Caregivers need similar information and families should be encouraged to send notes back. A "Back-and-Forth Notebook" can be used to share two-way information. This is particularly effective when caregivers and the family are working toward a specific goal with a child, whether introducing a new food or beginning toilet training. Parents can report on any progress made or problems encountered. Encourage parents to keep the team aware of important events that can influence a child's behavior: a toddler's sleepless night, a teething baby, exposure to a contagious illness, a death in the family, as well as happy events like getting a new toy, a visiting relative, or a new pregnancy.

This back-and-forth information sharing does more than transmit important data; it also strengthens the sense of teamwork between caregivers and families.

## Parent Bulletin Boards

Bulletin boards are another informal means of communication with parents. Post notices of meetings, information sheets on child development, nutrition, and other topics of interest to parents. Volunteer sign-up sheets and instructions for helpers can also be posted. Since young infants should be on their own internal schedules, an individual chart, with the infant's photo on it, can be posted with the baby's daily routines and schedule noted. News should be posted about any special events, such as field trips, special visitors, and birthdays. It is important to make the bulletin boards bright and cheerful and to change them frequently.

Bulletin boards display children's art, stories about field trips, or photographs of siblings and other family members. Be creative. Let the bulletin boards communicate the atmosphere and activities of the classroom. Ask families to contribute to the bulletin boards. Ask an artistic parent to come to the classroom and draw or paint with the children, then post the children's artwork on the bulletin board.

## Videos

If available, cameras and video cameras are a powerful way to show parents what their children do during the day. Parents feel more involved when they see a photograph or videotape of their child as he plays or learns a new skill. Videotapes of activities and events can also be used at parent meetings to show different aspects of the program or to illustrate development. Always request parents' permission to have their children taped or picture taken. Some programs obtain written parental permission at the time of enrollment to videotape or photograph their children at any time during the year.

## Newsletters

Newsletters or news sheets are another good way to communicate with families. Sending a newsletter home with a child on a regular (preferably biweekly or monthly) schedule ensures that all families receive the same information. The intent and topics of the newsletters may vary. Mention children and family members as often as appropriate, and be sure to include everyone over time. Suggested topics for newsletters include the following:

- Announcements of a meeting, event, or community trip
- Requests for materials or help with a project
- Information about community resources or events
- Child-centered topics: health, nutrition, physical growth, language, motor, and social/emotional development
- The current focus of the classroom
- Suggestions for at-home activities

- Thank-you notes to volunteers
- Requests for volunteers

Newsletters should be short and easy to read; brief, frequent newsletters are more effective than long, infrequent ones. Distribute newsletters on a regular basis, using a similar format each time, and write clearly, avoiding jargon.

## Home Visits

High-quality infant and toddler programs usually schedule home visits twice a year, the first time shortly after the child is enrolled and the second time toward the end of the school year. Home visits are a good way to establish rapport with families, reassure them about your interest in their child, and begin the process of two-way communication. The purposes of the visit are to get acquainted with the family, ask about the child's general health and development, his interests and needs, and discuss important issues such as toileting, feeding, temperament, and sleeping patterns. Toddlers enjoy showing their teacher their room, special toys, pets, and other important possessions.

Home visits can be rewarding for both the teaching team and families. The caregiver can learn more about the family's culture, its preferences, interactions, communication styles, and any special skills or talents that a family member might be willing to share with the program. The caregiver has uninterrupted time to concentrate on a discussion of that child's progress and successes. The family gets the personal attention of the caregiver and can see how the caregiver and their child interact. Parents have an unhurried opportunity to discuss concerns, misunderstandings, or their specific goals for their child. If both the family and the caregiver are clear about the purpose and intent, home visits can establish and maintain good communication which will enhance the child's and family's experience in the program.

Both caregivers and families sometimes feel a little intimidated by the suggestion of a home visit. However, if it is approached as a visit to an acquaintance's home and all the manners and behaviors associated with visiting someone in their home are observed, it will go smoothly. You may want to bring a new, inexpensive toy for the child to play with while you talk with the family.

Always schedule the visit at a convenient time for the family, when all the adults that the child lives with be home. Explain the purpose of the visit and how long it will last. Families may worry that a visit means bad news, so be clear that the purpose is to get better acquainted and to learn more about the child and family. Start the visit by repeating the purpose of the visit. Referring to a copy of the toddler's daily schedule or an infant's daily report form will get the conversation started. Always begin the discussion by saying something positive. Leave a written copy of important information that parents can review after the visit. Don't do all the talking. Always leave time for families to talk about the children and their ideas, concerns, and interests. Practice active listening techniques. Do not talk about the toddlers in their presence unless it is to give honest praise or other positive feedback. If you have concerns or problems to raise, arrange for someone to play with the child in another room or save the concern for a private meeting at the school.

## Involving Families

There are many ways families can be actively involved in the program. Some families may attend meetings, others may send materials from home, others may offer to work on the playground or be on the advisory committee. Some family members may volunteer to work in the center helping to cook, do laundry, answer the telephone, or work with the children in the classroom.

### Families in the Classroom

Parents often feel uncomfortable in the classroom because they think of it as the caregiver's domain and are not sure what to do. Parents must feel confident that they are welcome in the program anytime. When they arrive, greet parents by name, tell them where to put their personal belongings, and show them what to do. This kind of personal attention helps ease any awkwardness a parent may be feeling. Parents who are helping for the first time will need guidance, reassurance, and a "thank you" so they will feel good about their contribution and want to return.

There are many creative ways to help parents understand what to do in the classroom. At first it is important to give them specific tasks, like rocking or feeding a baby or joining two toddlers as they make things out of playdough. As parents become more comfortable in the classroom they will take cues from the children and be comfortable playing with them.

Knowing the rules and specific procedures of the program reassures parents. Parents should receive a written copy of classroom rules when their child is first enrolled in the program. At the beginning of each year, caregivers should explain program procedures to families and also post written copies on the Parent Bulletin Board. The procedures can include techniques for diapering, feeding, and naptime. When this information is easily available for a quick review, family members are more likely to feel confident and willing to return to the classroom. Always thank family members for coming and remind them to ask if they have any questions.

Both caregivers and families benefit when families participate in classroom activities. As family members become familiar with the team, they will feel more comfortable discussing their child's development and their own concerns. They will begin to feel a sense of ownership in the program and develop friendships with other parents. Participating in the classroom helps parents understand child development, introduces them to activities they can do at home, gives answers to unasked questions, and is an opportunity to observe their child playing and communicating with other children and adults.

Parents who participate in classroom activities on a regular basis should be subject to the same health requirements that staff must follow, including periodic physical examinations on a set schedule, tuberculin tests, and full immunizations.

## Family Room

A space that is dedicated to families immediately says, "Welcome, we want you here." Whether this is shared space or a separate room, an attractive area designated for families provides many options for family involvement. The room should have a sofa or comfortable chairs and a rug. If possible, have coffee or tea available as well as simple snack food. A comfortable rocking chair makes it easy for mothers to breast-feed or fathers to rock their babies. A refrigerator to store breast milk should also be available. Post children's drawings or pictures of infants and toddlers to create a feeling of home. A box filled with toys appropriate for infants, toddlers, and preschoolers provides entertainment for brothers and sisters.

Family members should always feel welcome in the Family Room. They can visit with other parents, read the information displayed on the bulletin board, or simply relax with a cup of tea. It is important that the Family Room be available for parents at regular times each day. If the room also serves as an office for staff, it may be necessary to schedule times during the day when the room is closed. Update the room schedule weekly and post it where everyone can see it. This room is an important part of a family participation initiative and should be open to families as much as possible. If the Family Room is also used for parent meetings and other group events, folding chairs should be available.

## Community Room

A space that families can use to share or exchange clothes, toys, and household items is a welcome resource. If a separate room is not available, space can be set aside in the Family Room. Sewing machines for families' personal and program use are often popular. If the space is available in the evenings or on weekends, families can use it for social events and work projects.

Social service agencies in the community may want to use the Community Room to meet with families or distribute information. Whenever possible, encourage their use of the space.

## Lending Library

A supply of age-appropriate toys and children's books as well as parenting books and pamphlets about child growth and development should be available for parents to borrow. Parents and children share a special time as they read age-appropriate children's books together or play a game. If parenting books are not available, teachers can write information sheets on child- and parent-centered topics for parents to read.

The Lending Library is usually located in the Family Room. Use a sign-up sheet or individual cards to record who has borrowed a toy and when it will be returned. In general, families can sign out toys for two to three weeks and then return the toys so another family can use them. Families can borrow toys as often as they wish.

It is important for families to feel comfortable borrowing toys and books, so make it clear that families need to care for materials, but accidents do happen. Remove broken toys from use because they can be dangerous. Repair broken toys and mend torn books if at all possible. Parents are often very good at fixing things, and that may be one way they can contribute to the program. Toys should not be loaned to another family until they have been sanitized.

## Involving Fathers

Every effort should be made to include and make welcome the men who are important in the infants' and toddlers' lives. Because initial contacts are often with mothers, the fathers, brothers, uncles, grandfathers, and male friends could be unintentionally left out. Encourage them to attend meetings and participate in program activities.

Ask when both parents can be available and schedule the visit or conference for that time. Include the men in all discussions. Ask them questions about the child. Address notes and invitations to both fathers and mothers. If reports need to be signed, ask for both signatures. This tells the father "You are important to us."

Several strategies are recommended for including fathers in the program:

- Ask the men how they would like to contribute to the program. They may have building talents, enjoy outdoor work, or be willing to help with community activities.

- Plan social events for the men to get together, talk about their children, share concerns, and exchange ideas.

- Offer parenting classes just for men, led by a man, if possible. Emphasize ways men can enjoy being with their infants and toddlers. Fathers' classes sometimes develop into peer support groups and can be very beneficial.

- Sponsor social events like family evenings or shared meals that encourage participation of both fathers and mothers as well as other family members.

## Family Meetings and Gatherings

Family meetings and gatherings are an important part of the program. Most centers hold several types of meetings, including regularly scheduled parent meetings, advisory committee meetings, support groups, informal gatherings, and celebrations.

*Parent Meetings* Team members are responsible for scheduling parent meetings, which are usually held once a month, and provide a time to discuss program matters and topics of mutual concern. Program staff or an outside speaker presents information and promotes discussion on the chosen topic. The families, teachers, and administrators together choose the topics and agree on the most convenient time to meet. If meetings are to benefit parents, they must cover issues that interest parents. Just as child-centered learning works best, so does parent-centered learning. Parents are unlikely to attend meetings that are not useful, informative, and reasonably convenient.

Find out what interests families either through informal discussion or by using the interest survey. Topics like infant and toddler growth and development are usually presented in a formal way, followed by a question and answer period. Other subjects are best covered in participatory sessions when families can practice new skills and techniques.

Some topics of interest to families include the following:

- Life with a new baby
- Infants' and toddlers' sleeping patterns
- Reading infants cues and body language
- Childhood nutrition
- Childhood diseases and safety
- Understanding siblings' reactions to a new baby
- Playing with infants and toddlers
- Feeding infants and toddlers
- Where to find support in the community

**Support Groups** Families with new babies often have similar questions and concerns. They benefit from being able to talk with other families, share experiences, and problem solve together. Support groups usually form out of a common need to cope with a particular issue. After hearing a presentation on a specific topic, parents often want more information. Families who share a common concern can offer each other support, suggestions, or resources. Support groups can be for fathers only, single parents, parents of children who have disabilities, new parents, or mothers. Staff should encourage these groups as much as possible by providing meeting space and coffee.

**Social Events** Social events or gatherings are opportunities for families to have fun, share experiences, talk with other families, and feel that they are a part of the program. Families and staff collaborate to plan and organize morning coffees, informal chats in the Family Room, field or community trips, picnics, family dinners, holiday parties, and game nights. These activities may be planned in collaboration with other classrooms.

***Celebrations*** Everyone likes to feel appreciated, so it is important to acknowledge and celebrate successes. This is the first experience away from home for infants and toddlers and their families. The children's accomplishments should be celebrated. Family members volunteer valuable time to the program. They deserve thanks and recognition.

Families and staff build the program and their partnerships over time and in many ways. Families contribute to the program by attending meetings, donating materials, assisting in the classroom, and helping to build equipment or clean up the outdoor area. Thank everyone for their participation.

***Family Advisory Committee*** A Family Advisory Committee formally empowers parents to contribute ideas on all aspects of the program, from planning to implementation. Parents learn to plan and facilitate meetings, campaign for election, hold office, raise funds, work with committees, and plan strategically.

All families, not just Committee members, should be invited to attend the meetings, which are usually held every three months. Topics commonly addressed include the following:

- Family participation
- Parent-teacher communication
- Community involvement
- Social events
- Fund raising events

The team must be responsive to the recommendations of the committee, and have sound reasons for not implementing recommendations and suggestions. The Step by Step administrator works closely with the officers of the advisory committee and, as a team, they solve problems and generate new initiatives.

# Confidentiality

Confidentiality is of the utmost importance if families and caregivers are to trust, respect, and work together in the best interests of the children. Staff should encourage an atmosphere of open discussion and provide many opportunities for families to talk privately about issues regarding their children or a troubling family situation. Offer places to speak privately with parents and always regard the information as confidential. Every Step by Step Program must have a written policy on confidentiality and all staff and families must know about it and follow it in the most professional manner.

All efforts to build a supportive program can be undone if confidential information is divulged about children, parents, or staff. Keep records in a locked file and create a check-out system for the few key staff who have reason and permission to use the records.

Furthermore, a family is required to give written permission before staff can disclose information to others. Families must know how and what information may be shared, and they must have the right to review their child's file at any time.

## SAMPLE LETTER

Dear Mr. and Mrs. _____:

We are delighted that your child will be enrolled in the Step by Step Infant and Toddler Program this year. We look forward to creating a partnership with you and your child. As you know, we encourage families to be involved in our program as much as possible. We want to know how you would like to be involved. Please look at the enclosed Family Interest Survey and check those items that interest you. If we have not included something that is of interest to you, please let us know.

We look forward to seeing you soon and getting to know you in the months ahead.

Thank you.

# FAMILY INTEREST SURVEY

Child's Name: _____

Parents' Names: _____

Caregivers: _____

| *We are interested in:* | *Mother* | *Father* |
|---|---|---|
| Attending monthly parent meeting | _____ | _____ |
| Working in the classroom with toddlers | _____ | _____ |

(If checked, what activities would you prefer?)

| | | |
|---|---|---|
| Reading | _____ | _____ |
| Art | _____ | _____ |
| Music | _____ | _____ |
| Building or making materials (outdoor equipment, doll clothes, games) | _____ | _____ |
| Helping with community trips | _____ | _____ |
| Planning special events (birthdays, holidays) | _____ | _____ |
| Sending materials from home | _____ | _____ |
| Attending/planning events for families | _____ | _____ |
| Joining a parent group | _____ | _____ |
| Helping with a lending library | _____ | _____ |
| Contributing toys | _____ | _____ |
| Other: _____ | _____ | _____ |

# CHILD INFORMATION SHEET

**PHOTO**

My name is_____

I was born on _____

I am _____ months old.

My family includes

_____
_____
_____
_____
_____

We live at

_____
_____
_____
_____

Phone:

_____

In case of emergency, contact:

1._____
Phone:_____
2._____
Phone:_____
3._____
Phone:_____

# WHAT YOU SHOULD KNOW ABOUT ME

My name is: _____

I like to eat!!

What:

_____
_____
_____

When:

_____
_____
_____

Allergies:

_____
_____
_____

My nap schedule is:

_____
_____

Special information:

_____
_____

My favorite toys and games are:

_____
_____

I am happy when:

_____
_____

I get scared when:

_____
_____

Other important things everyone who cares for me should know:

_____

A sample form for parents:

# "WHAT I DID TODAY..."

DATE:_____

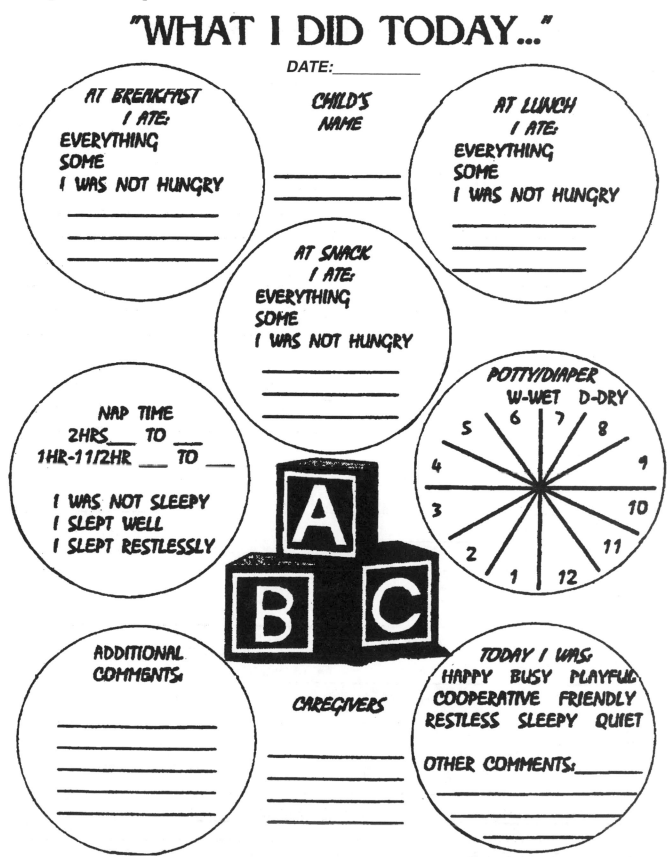

CHILD'S NAME
_____

AT BREAKFAST I ATE:
EVERYTHING
SOME
I WAS NOT HUNGRY
_____
_____
_____

AT LUNCH I ATE:
EVERYTHING
SOME
I WAS NOT HUNGRY
_____
_____
_____

AT SNACK I ATE:
EVERYTHING
SOME
I WAS NOT HUNGRY
_____
_____
_____

NAP TIME
2HRS___ TO ___
1HR-1 1/2HR ___ TO ___

I WAS NOT SLEEPY
I SLEPT WELL
I SLEPT RESTLESSLY

POTTY/DIAPER
W-WET   D-DRY

ADDITIONAL COMMENTS:
_____
_____
_____
_____
_____

CAREGIVERS
_____
_____
_____

TODAY I WAS:
HAPPY   BUSY   PLAYFUL
COOPERATIVE   FRIENDLY
RESTLESS   SLEEPY   QUIET

OTHER COMMENTS:_____
_____
_____
_____

# DAILY INFORMATION SHEET

Date:

Form filled out by:

_____

Baby's Name:

_____

Feedings:

_____
_____
_____
_____

Sleeping:

_____
_____
_____
_____

Diapering/Toileting:

_____
_____
_____
_____

Other:

_____
_____
_____

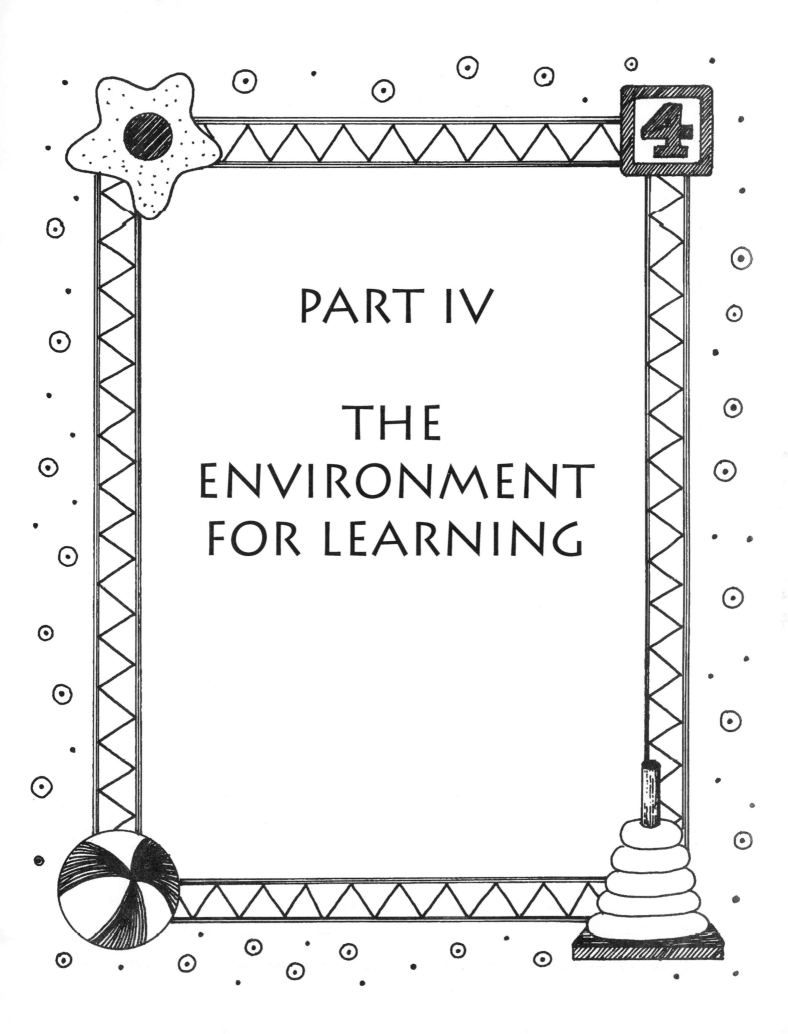

PART IV

THE
ENVIRONMENT
FOR LEARNING

# CHAPTER 12

# ENSURING A HEALTHY ENVIRONMENT

# 12. ENSURING A HEALTHY ENVIRONMENT

The health and safety of children are essential priorities of a quality infant and toddler program. Its caregivers act to prevent illness and accidents and are prepared for emergencies. The information in this chapter is not meant to replace official health regulations. It is meant to present the current best practices to guide caregivers. This chapter discusses practices necessary to a healthy environment as they relate to:

- Maintaining the physical surroundings
- Developing policies and procedures: the Health Handbook
- Preventing the spread of germs
- Monitoring children's health
- Using health professionals as resources

The health needs of infants and toddlers require a well trained, vigilant staff, and close supervision. Because infants and toddlers are at the peak of their sensory and motor explorations and almost everything goes into their mouths, the size and cleanliness of toys must be evaluated carefully. The children must be in view at all times so that staff can reach them quickly to prevent accidents. The environment must accommodate children's active learning, be flexible enough to meet children's individual needs, and provide opportunities for exploration and discovery.

## The Physical Surroundings

Buildings, grounds, and equipment should be clean, repaired, and maintained to protect the health of children. Lighting, ventilation, and heat must be adequate. Both natural and artificial light should be used in classrooms, halls, and stairways. Lighting is important to health because it is a major source of sensory stimulation.

Fresh air is also important to good health. Build outdoor time into the daily schedule. Windows and doors should be opened during the day to refresh the rooms. A ventilating system can help to maintain adequate circulation of air. Heating and ventilating systems should be checked annually to ensure that they are working properly, as their filters can be breeding grounds for bacteria. Rugs should be checked for dampness, and dehumidifiers should be used where dampness is a problem.

To keep the building free of insects and rodents, provide screens for exterior windows and doors. Post instructions for the safe and proper use of pesticides or other chemicals. Label and store all chemicals, cleaning supplies, and pesticides in locked areas, away from children, and food preparation and serving areas. Wash reusable napkins, bibs, and table cloths after each use.

All adults who work in the center (teachers, assistants, cooks, cleaners, and parent volunteers) must have a complete physical examination, including all immunizations appropriate to adults and a tuberculosis screening, when they are hired and regularly thereafter.

The center should be free of cigarette smoke. Because an increasing body of evidence links children's respiratory problems with passive smoke, caregivers should refrain from smoking near children and should educate parents about the risks.

## Policies and Procedures: The Health Handbook

Each program should have a *written* handbook of health procedures for staff and parents, developed cooperatively by the staff, parents, and health consultants. While general guidelines are offered in this text, a copy of *The ABCs of Safe and Healthy Child Care: A Handbook for Child Care Providers*, published by the Centers for Disease Control and Prevention and the Department of Health and Human Services, may be downloaded free from their website (www.cdc.gov). This publication offers detailed health guidelines for child care programs.

Staff and volunteer parents must be trained in health procedures. Policies and procedures should identify who will do what, when, where, and how, and should include information on the following:

- Maintaining health records
- Reporting and managing infectious diseases
- Preventing injuries
- Providing first aid
- Preparing for emergencies
- Monitoring infection control procedures
- Giving medications

- Planning for individual health needs
- Providing health and safety training for staff, children, and parents

Once the procedures are developed, standard procedures for diapering, feeding, and handwashing should be posted as a reminder to staff, visitors, and volunteers.

## *Preventing the Spread of Germs*

### Handwashing

Cleanliness deters disease. The benefits of washing hands cannot be overemphasized. Many infections are caused by germs transmitted by hand-to-hand contact. Handwashing removes germs and is the single most effective method of preventing the spread of communicable diseases to other children, staff, or family members. Caregivers should wash their hands when they enter the infant and toddler care area, and before and after:

- Feeding
- Diapering or toileting
- Giving medications
- Bathing
- Nose-blowing
- Handling pets
- Any special care procedure

Infants and toddlers scratch and touch infected areas, thereby transmitting germs from hand to mouth, and to toys. If the caregiver does not wash the baby's hands, she will infect herself or other children. Make handwashing a time of enjoyment—sing a song or hum a tune. Infants and toddlers should wash their hands before eating, after toileting, after touching or handling anything that is dirty, or after playing outdoors. Children must be taught why it is important to wash their hands and how to do it properly.

165

## RECOMMENDED HANDWASHING PROCEDURES

- Wash hands for two minutes at start and end of day.
- Wash hands for at least one minute after feeding, diapering or toileting, giving medications, bathing, nose-blowing, handling pets, or any special care procedure.
- Use running water.
- Use soap. Liquid soap is preferred.
- Stand in front of the sink. Wet your hands and arms above wrists.
- Rub vigorously, using circular movements to wash palms, backs of hands and the lower arms. (The friction helps to remove the germs.)
- Rinse hands well under running water until all soil and soap is gone.
- Avoid germs on the faucet by using a towel to turn it off.
- Use a disposable towel to dry hands. If paper towels are not available, use a clean cloth towel.
- Throw paper towels in a lined, covered trash container. Put used cloth towels in a covered container so that they can be laundered before being used again.

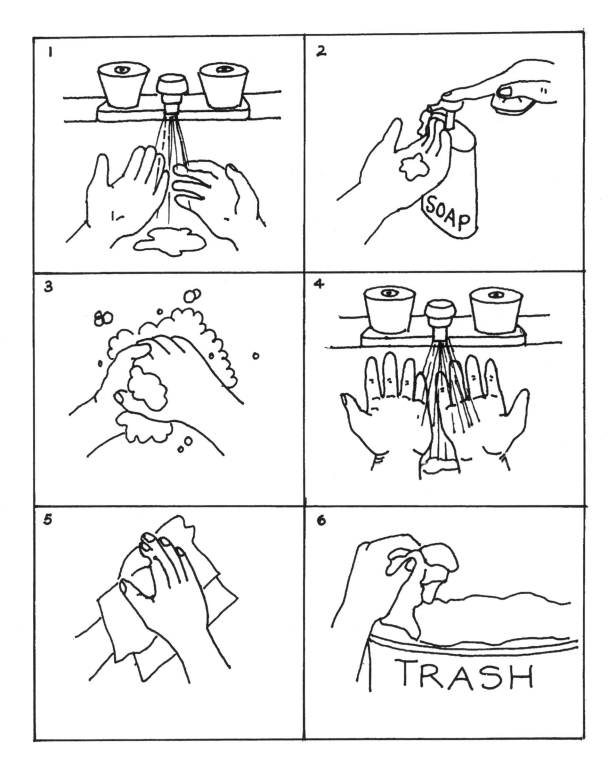

## Sanitation

Most parents and pediatricians agree that preventing the spread of contagious childhood ailments is a difficult task. Fighting the spread of infections among brothers, sisters, and other family members is especially challenging because they have frequent contact with each other and share toys and other objects. Children who spend their day in an infant and toddler program are at even greater risk for the spread of germs as they interact with each other, put toys in their mouths, touch each other, use communal toilets and sinks, and play together. The challenge for caregivers is to do everything possible to keep children safe and healthy while encouraging them to explore their surroundings and interact with others.

Contagious illnesses are caused by either viral or bacterial infections. Tiny bacterial organisms live in our bodies and environment and thrive on wet surfaces, such as sinks and areas where food is prepared and stored. Viruses spread from person to person by coughing, sneezing, touching, and handling contaminated objects. Most childhood illnesses are viral in nature, including diarrhea, chicken pox, conjunctivitis, colds, and influenza. A description of their symptoms and what parents should watch for should be included in the educational materials and training offered to parents.

Sanitary classroom surroundings and materials are extremely important because infants and toddlers investigate toys, furniture, pets, and each other by touching and tasting. Careful sanitary practices reduce the spread of infections and diseases.

While cleaning removes germs, sanitizing actually kills the germs. All surfaces and toys can be safely disinfected with a bleach and water mixture. For surfaces such as bathrooms and diapering areas, use 1/4 cup of bleach per gallon of cool water. A weaker solution of 1 tbsp bleach to 1 gallon of cool water should be used for disinfecting toys and eating utensils (Center for Disease Control, 1996). A fresh mixture of bleach and water must be made daily and clearly labeled because it weakens and loses its effectiveness when exposed to air.

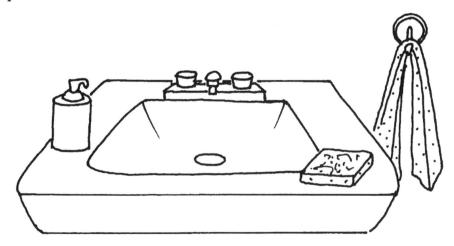

The most effective way to fight germs is to scrub hands, toys, play surfaces, cribs and cots, and diaper-changing areas frequently with bacteria-fighting soap. (Store used toys in separate bins until they can be cleaned.)

- Wash napkins, bibs, and table cloths after each use.
- Launder wet mops and cleaning cloths daily.
- Clean furniture surfaces and toys daily.
- Clean and mop kitchen and bathroom floors daily, or more often when soiled.
- Dust walls daily and wash them at least once a week.
- Move carpeting daily to inhibit moisture.
- Vacuum carpets each evening and shampoo them every four weeks.
- Keep the classrooms, halls, and stairways neat, clean, and free of unnecessary items.
- Store garbage in water- and rodent-proof containers with tight lids. Stainless steel or hard rubber trash cans with lockable lids are preferred.
- Remove trash containers from the children's areas daily, or more often if necessary.

If a child brings a favorite toy or pacifier from home, it must be kept in his crib. Label individual teething toys and keep them separate. Children's blankets should be clearly labeled and used by the same child from one day to the next.

---

### RECOMMENDED SANITIZING PROCEDURES

- Clean dirty surfaces and objects with soap and water.
- Make a new mixture of bleach and water each day.
- Apply the mixture to large objects with a hand-spray; dip smaller objects into the bleach/water mixture.
- Air-dry toys and surfaces before using them.

---

## Diapering and Toileting

When diapering, lay the child on a clean surface that is disinfected after each use or on a disposable covering that is changed after each use. Children should have individual diapering materials that are not shared. Until they can be laundered, dispose of soiled diapers in closed containers out of reach of children. Soiled diapers should be laundered daily. A sink with hot and cold water should be very close to diapering and toileting areas.

Toilet facilities must be kept clean and sanitized. If potty chairs are used, they should be in good condition and easily cleanable. Wash, rinse, and sanitize the potty chair bowl in a sink designated for this purpose only.

The toilet area needs to be sanitized daily or as needed during the day. Sinks and toilets should be either child-sized or made accessible by non-slip stools. Soap and disposable towels should be available at all sinks. All of the above diapering and toileting procedures should be posted for staff to see.

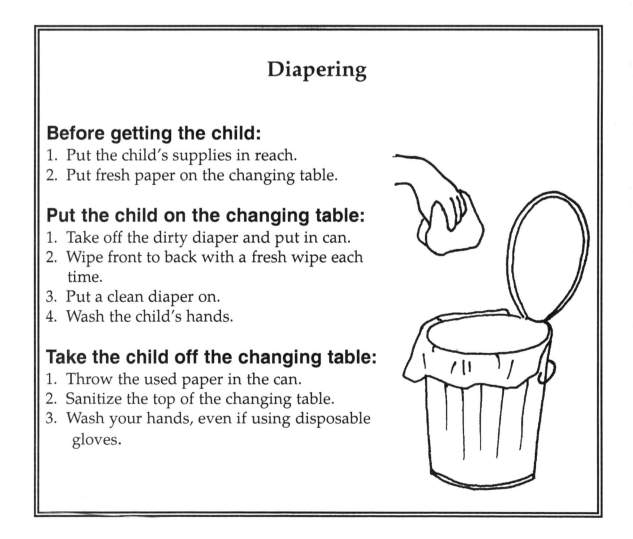

## Diapering

### Before getting the child:
1. Put the child's supplies in reach.
2. Put fresh paper on the changing table.

### Put the child on the changing table:
1. Take off the dirty diaper and put in can.
2. Wipe front to back with a fresh wipe each time.
3. Put a clean diaper on.
4. Wash the child's hands.

### Take the child off the changing table:
1. Throw the used paper in the can.
2. Sanitize the top of the changing table.
3. Wash your hands, even if using disposable gloves.

## Checklist for a Healthy Environment

Use these questions as guides to design and maintain a healthy environment for infants and toddlers.

√ Are walls, floors, rugs, mops, and linens cleaned according to the schedule?
√ Are the surface areas and toilet areas washed and disinfected daily?
√ Are toys cleaned daily in a light bleach solution?
√ Are teething toys individually labeled with infants' names?
√ Is carpeting removed from the floor daily to inhibit moisture?
√ Are storage bins available to store toys that need to be cleaned? (For example, toys mouthed by infants)
√ Are food preparation, feeding, diapering, and toileting areas cleaned after every use?
√ Are the diapering and feeding areas separated?
√ Are foods safely stored to prevent spoilage?
√ Does each child have individual diapering materials that are not shared?
√ Are soiled diapers and clothes placed in closed containers or sealed in labeled plastic bags?
√ Are procedures posted for diaper changing, feeding, and hand washing?
√ Are hot and cold water available near the diapering and feeding areas?
√ Do adults wash their hands thoroughly before and after diapering and feeding?
√ Are infants' hands washed? Are toddlers taught and encouraged to wash their hands?
√ Are procedures for health emergencies posted in a prominent place?
√ Are procedures written for the care of sick children, maintenance of health records, and dispensing medications?
√ Are staff trained in health procedures?

## *Monitoring Children's Health*

Knowledge about child growth and development and individual differences between children helps caregivers understand the children's multiple needs. In a high quality program, the caregivers (1) are alert to each child's health status and any changes in that status, (2) record and report individual health concerns and accidents to other staff and parents, and (3) follow written health policies and procedures.

### Individual Health Records

Up-to-date written records that include the following items should be maintained for each child:

- A complete health evaluation by an approved health care provider
- A record of immunizations
- A list of any current medications
- Emergency contact information
- Names of people authorized to act on behalf of the child
- Allergies, chronic conditions, and developmental issues

A sample *Child Health Information Questionnaire* is available at the end of this chapter.

Each morning as caregivers greet children, they should make a brief health check and be alert to changes in activity levels, breathing difficulties, rashes, swellings, bruises, sores, and discharges from nose, ears, or eyes. As parents drop off their children, the caregiver should inquire about these changes.

### Immunizations

It is essential that all children be fully immunized against the main childhood infections including diphtheria, tetanus, pertussis, polio, measles, mumps, rubella, and haemophilas influenza, type B (HIB). (See the *Recommended Childhood Immunization Schedule* at the end of this chapter.)

### Policies and Procedures for Sick Children and Caregivers

Written policies and procedures about caring for sick children include procedures for the notification of parents, the comfort of ill children and staff, and the protection of well children. The American Academy of Pediatrics recommends that the policies be developed in consultation with community health care specialists and physicians, and should consider the physical facilities as well as the number and qualifications of the program's personnel. Parents should receive a copy of the program's health policies when they enroll the child in the program.

When a child becomes ill during the day, separate him from the other children. Comfort him, call his parents, and follow basic practices of care for the symptoms. The classroom should have a Get Well Area where a child can rest or play quietly. It should be accessible so that a caregiver can quietly administer to the physical and emotional needs of the sick child. The caregivers need to be able to see the area and the child at all times. If the child needs to be in a totally separate area because of intestinal or respiratory problems, an adult must be with him at all times.

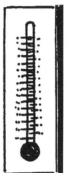

*If an infant under four months of age has a rectal temperature of 101 degrees Fahrenheit or higher, or an older infant has a rectal temperature of 102 degrees Fahrenheit or higher, call the parents immediately and seek medical attention.*

As they develop policies and procedures for the care of sick children, staff should ask the following questions:

- Does the program have enough staff and separate space to care for a mildly ill child who needs some individual attention?
- Is there a space where the mildly ill child can rest?
- Is the space arranged so that all children can be observed carefully?

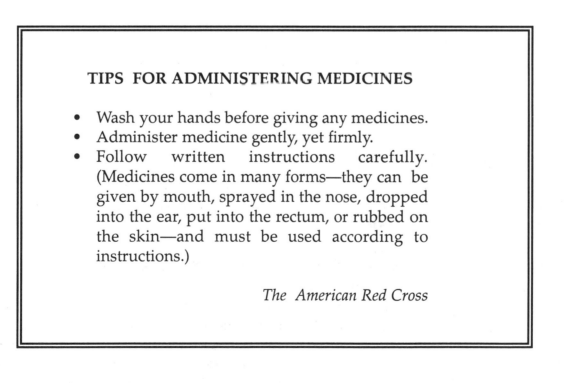

**TIPS FOR ADMINISTERING MEDICINES**

- Wash your hands before giving any medicines.
- Administer medicine gently, yet firmly.
- Follow written instructions carefully. (Medicines come in many forms—they can be given by mouth, sprayed in the nose, dropped into the ear, put into the rectum, or rubbed on the skin—and must be used according to instructions.)

*The American Red Cross*

## Medications

Most children require medications at one time or another and the caregiver may be asked to administer the medications. Written policy should state clearly who is responsible for administering medications. Before agreeing to give any medication, whether prescription or over-the-counter, obtain written permission from the parents. A permanent medication log should be kept, as well as individual medication records that are placed in each child's health folder. Both the medication log and the individual records should include the following information:

- Name of the child to whom the medicine was given
- Name of the medication
- Date, time, and amount of medication given
- Name of the person who administered the medication

*The medication must be administered to the child as stated on the label directions or as amended by a physician and requires written parental permission.*

Any medications brought by parents for their children must meet the following criteria:

- If prescribed medication, include the name of the prescribing physician
- Be in the original container
- Be labeled with the child's first and last name
- Include directions to store and administer the medication
- Be labeled with the date the prescription was filled
- Have an expiration date
- Be in a child-proof container

*Medications must be kept out of reach of children or in locked storage. If refrigeration is required, medications must be kept separate from food.*

## *Using Health Professionals as Resources*

Staff at each infant and toddler center should be knowledgeable about the medical resources available within the community. In many countries, local health professionals are assigned to the center. Many clinics have staff who can help develop program guidelines and policies and are usually available to help train parents and staff. Local hospitals, colleges, clinics, or other community agencies may also provide additional staff, information, and assistance. Caregivers cannot be experts in all areas of medical need. However, they can become aware of the resources of health educators, physicians, parents, nutritionists, mental health specialists, special education teachers, and other community health agencies that may assist families.

## *A Reminder*

Planning ahead for emergencies and illnesses prepares the staff for most situations. The infant and toddler center that carefully prevents health hazards, develops written procedures, and trains its staff and parents in sound health practices, ensures a healthy and safe environment, one that supports children as they grow, play, learn, and thrive.

# Recommended Childhood Immunization Schedule
# United States, January - December 2000

*Vaccines[1] are listed under the routinely recommended ages. Bars indicate range of recommended ages for immunization. Any dose not given at the recommended age should be given as a "catch-up" immunization at any subsequent visit when indicated and feasible. Approved by the Advisory Committee on Immunization Practices (ACIP), the American Academy of Pediatrics (AAP), and the American Academy of Family Physicians (AAFP)*

| Age →<br>Vaccine ↓ | Birth | 1<br>month | 2<br>months | 4<br>months | 6<br>months | 12<br>months | 15<br>months | 18<br>months |
|---|---|---|---|---|---|---|---|---|
| Hepatitis B[2] | Hep B | Hep B | | | | | | |
| | | | Hep B | | | Hep B | | |
| Diptheria, Tetanus, Pertussis[3] | | | DTaP | DTaP | DTaP | | DTaP[3] | |
| H. Influenzae type b[4] | | | Hib | Hib | Hib | Hib | | |
| Polio[5] | | | IPV | IPV | IPV[5] | | | |
| Measles, Mumps, Rubella[5] | | | | | | MMR | | |
| Varicella[6] | | | | | | Var | | |

*On October 22, 1999, the Advisory Committee on Immunization Practices (ACIP) recommended that Rotashield (RRV-TV), the only U.S.-licensed rotavirus vaccine, no longer be used in the United States (MMWR, Volume 48, Number 43, Nov. 5, 1999). Parents should be reassured that their children who received rotavirus vaccine before July are not at increased risk for intussusception now.*

[1] *This schedule indicates the recommended ages for routine administration of currently licensed childhood vaccines as of 11/I/99. Additional vaccines may be licensed and recommended during the year. Licensed combination vaccines may be used whenever any components of the combination are indicated and its other components are not contraindicated. Providers should consult the manufacturers' package inserts for detailed recommendations.*

[2] *Infants born to HBsAg-negative mothers should receive the 1st dose of hepatitis B (Hep B) vaccine by age 2 months. The 2nd dose should be at least one month after the 1st dose. The 3rd dose should be administered at least 4 months after the 1st dose and at least 2 months after the 2nd dose, but not before 6 months of age for infants.*
*Infants born to HBsAg-positive mothers should receive hepatitis B vaccine and 0.5 mL hepatitis B immune globulin (HBIG) within 12 hours of birth at separate sites. The 2nd dose is recommended at 1-2 months of age and the 3rd dose at 6 months of age.*
*Infants born to mothers whose HBsAg status is unknown should receive hepatitis B vaccine within 12 hours of birth. Maternal blood should be drawn at the time of delivery to determine the mother's HBsAg status; if the HBsAg test is positive, the infant should receive HBIG as soon as possible (no later than 1 week of age).*
*All children and adolescents (through 18 years of age) who have not been immunized against hepatitis B may begin the series during any visit. Special efforts should be made to immunize children who were born in or whose parents were born in areas of the world with moderate or high endemicity of hepatitis B virus infection.*

*Please see Appendix C for complete notes.*
*Source: Centers for Disease Control and Prevention (CDC); reprinted with permission.*

# CHILD HEALTH INFORMATION QUESTIONNAIRE

Please take the time to complete this form.  The information will help us to know your child better and respond appropriately to his/her needs.

**Family Information**

Today's date: _____

Recorded by: _____

1.    Child's name:        (first) _____ (last) _____

"Pet" name, nickname _____

2.     Child's address: _____

_____

Home telephone number: _____

3.    Mother's name: _____

Mother's home address (if different from above): _____

_____

Mother's home telephone number: _____

Mother's work address: _____

Mother's work number: _____    Fax: _____

4.    Father's name: _____

Father's address (if different from above): _____

_____

Father's home telephone number: _____

Father's work address: _____

Father's work number: _____    Fax: _____

5.  Emergency Contact: _____

    Relationship to the Child: _____

    Phone: _____ Fax: _____

6.  Child's sex (male or female): _____

7.  Child's date of birth: _____
                              (month)        (date)        (year)

8.  Other family members living at the child's address (names and ages of children): _____

    _____

9.  Previous child care/schools attended: _____

    _____

    _____

**Birth History**

10.  Child's weight at birth: _____

11.  Length of pregnancy (premature/full term, number of months): _____

12.  Were there any complications with the pregnancy or birth? If so, what? ___

     _____

13.  Did your child have any medical problems at or soon after birth? If so, what?

     _____

14.  Family physician's name: _____

     Family physician's address: _____

     Family physician's phone number: _____

15.  Pediatrician's name: _____

     Pediatrician's address: _____

     Pediatrician's phone number: _____

16.  Dentist's name: _____

     Dentist's address: _____

     Dentist's phone number: _____

**Health Status**

17.  Please give a complete history of your child's immunization schedule (this may need to be verified by your doctor).

| Immunization type | Date given |
|---|---|
|  |  |
|  |  |
|  |  |
|  |  |
|  |  |

18.  What infectious diseases has your child ever suffered from?  Please check boxes. (Circle yes or no and add date if yes.)

| | | | |
|---|---|---|---|
| measles | yes | no | Date:_____ |
| rheumatic fever | yes | no | Date:_____ |
| chicken pox | yes | no | Date:_____ |
| pneumonia | yes | no | Date:_____ |
| mumps | yes | no | Date:_____ |
| meningitis | yes | no | Date:_____ |
| whooping cough | yes | no | Date:_____ |
| others: | | | Date:_____ |

19. Has your child suffered any repeated infections (cold, flu, tonsillitis, etc.)? _____

    _____

20. Has your child ever received treatment in a hospital emergency room? _____

    If so, why? _____

    _____

21. Has your child ever been admitted to a hospital as an inpatient?  If so, why? _____

    _____

22. Does your child take any medication on a regular basis?  If so, what? _____

    _____

23. Please offer any information about your child's health check-ups.  Has your
    child recently been evaluated by any of the following?  (Circle Yes or No and
    add result if Yes.)

    | | | | |
    |---|---|---|---|
    | dental surgeon | yes | no | Result:_____ |
    | ophthalmic surgeon | yes | no | Result:_____ |
    | hearing specialist | yes | no | Result:_____ |
    | pediatrician | yes | no | Result:_____ |
    | other specialist | yes | no | Result:_____ |

24. Does your child have any known allergies?     Yes    No

    To what?_____

    Severity of reaction:_____

25. (a) Does your child have problems with any of the following?

    (Circle Yes or No and describe Yes.)

    | | | | |
    |---|---|---|---|
    | asthma | yes | no | Describe:_____ |
    | hay fever | yes | no | Describe:_____ |
    | skin sensitivity | yes | no | Describe:_____ |
    | reaction to the sun | yes | no | Describe:_____ |
    | warts | yes | no | Describe:_____ |

| | | | |
|---|---|---|---|
| dairy products | yes | no | Describe:_____ |
| constipation | yes | no | Describe:_____ |
| easy bruising | yes | no | Describe:_____ |
| concentration | yes | no | Describe:_____ |
| mood swings | yes | no | Describe:_____ |
| sleep | yes | no | Describe:_____ |
| spasms, twitches, tics | yes | no | Describe:_____ |
| habits | yes | no | Describe:_____ |

other_____

(b) Are there any genetic diseases in the family?_____

26. Does your child behave in any way that concerns you? If so, what?_____

_____

27. Has your child ever been exposed to any significant traumatic event (witnessed

violence, divorce in family, moving home, death of relative, etc.)?   Yes    No

Describe:_____

_____

28. Does your child play in a way that you would expect?    Yes    No

Describe:_____

29. Do you have any concerns about your child's speech, communication,

understanding? If so, what?_____

30. What is your child's height?_____

Weight?_____

Shoe size?_____

30. What is your child's feeding/eating pattern (number of meals, snacks, types of

food/milk/formula, attitude to eating)?_____

# HEALTH UPDATE

Name:_____ Today's Date:_____

Age/Date of Birth:_____

New immunizations (cross reference to immunization record card):

Immunization type                Date given

_____                _____

_____                _____

_____                _____

Recent health conditions:_____

Medication:_____

Physician's reports (attach if appropriate):_____

Updates on growth information

(also plot data in growth chart)

Height:_____

Weight:_____

Shoe size:_____

Identified health needs:_____

# HEALTH AND ILLNESS CHART

Name:                                             Birthdate:

Family Name:                                      Physician:

Diagnosed Conditions:                             Allergies:

Family Concerns:

| Date And Time | Behavior/Symptom | Description | Comment |
|---|---|---|---|
|  |  |  |  |

# INJURY REPORT FORM

Date of injury: _____

Time of injury: _____

Name of injured: _____

    Age:_____

Where injury happened: _____
_____

How injury happened: _____
_____
_____
_____

Part of body injured: _____

Objects involved (if any): _____

What was done to help the injured: _____
_____
_____
_____

Parent/Guardian advised:
    of injury:_____
    to seek medical attention:_____

Supervisor at time of injury: _____

Witness completing form: _____

(Centers for Disease Control and Prevention, 1996)

# CHAPTER 13

# ENSURING A SAFE ENVIRONMENT

# 13. ENSURING A SAFE ENVIRONMENT

Safety is essential to a carefully planned environment. Safe environments are designed to prevent accidents and injuries. This chapter gives the characteristics of a safe environment, including: indoor and outdoor safety, emergency first aid procedures and precautions, and useful safety checklists.

## Characteristics of a Safe Environment

In a safe environment children are free to move and explore their new and interesting world without the constant worry of caregivers. Because the environment is safe, the word "no" does not have to be used often and caregivers can relax as they talk and play with the children. The children gradually learn to protect themselves and look out for others.

Caregivers must always be alert to where the children are and what they are playing with. Staff should know basic first-aid procedures and should periodically check and monitor both indoor and outdoor environments for hazards and dangerous materials.

## Indoor Safety

One of the most effective general guidelines for ensuring a safe environment for infants and toddlers is never to assume the babies cannot do something. Babies are inquisitive and mobile. Never assume that it is safe to leave a three-month-old baby on a high surface because she cannot roll over or wiggle off—she can! As toddlers become mobile, they are constantly exploring things. Never assume that a twelve-month-old would not be interested in reaching for a cup of hot coffee on a table. It is best to assume that a baby will do all the things he is capable of—and probably more!

## "Baby-Proof" the Space

Accidents can happen even in the safest of environments. To "baby-proof" the infant and toddler room, get down on your knees and look around the environment to see it from the children's viewpoint. Do you see places where small heads, hands, or feet could get caught? Are there places a baby could crawl into and not be seen? Do you see stairs or ledges that are too steep? Are there any small toys that could choke a child?

Ask yourself if the children can play freely without harming themselves or others. Accidents usually occur either when a child attempts to do or get something beyond his capabilities and is not supervised properly. Young children do not understand dangers. Install gates to prevent children from moving into dangerous spaces, like stairs. Children from 12 to 24 months of age must be shown that certain behaviors or actions could cause injuries. By showing the children the stove is hot or electrical outlets are dangerous, they will begin to learn what to avoid and what not do. On the other hand, they need to attempt new activities and take risks safely. Aim for a balance between allowing children flexibility and movement, and restricting them with a non-responsive, over-protected environment.

## Dangerous Situations and Times

Infants and toddlers are more likely to have accidents at particular times of day or under certain situations. Staff should be especially alert to those circumstances when caregivers may be distracted and, as a result, children may be particularly accident-prone. Be alert to danger when:

- A staff member is absent or attending to other children
- A routine has been disrupted
- Parents and children are arriving or departing
- Staff are not aware of a child's current abilities

Each staff member should be responsible for certain children so that all children are being watched constantly. Staff may work together in zones at certain times of day, such as lunch or naptime.

---

**THE BEST RECOMMENDATION FOR CHILDREN'S SAFETY**

*Always* **be alert to the children.**

---

## Furniture and Equipment

Arrange furniture and equipment so that children and adults can move about freely, without bumping into things or being crowded. The furniture should be solid and stable or bolted to prevent tipping or falling. Keep chairs and other furniture away from windows and shelves to prevent children from climbing on them. Store toys and games on low shelves accessible to the children. Toys displayed on open shelves are inviting and encourage children to play.

Young children poke their fingers into everything. Cover hinges and joints to prevent pinched fingers and cover electrical outlets. Toddlers and mobile infants taste, lick, and put things into their mouths. Keep objects smaller than one and one quarter inches in diameter (approximately three centimeters) away from young children who are likely to mouth objects. Avoid toys, stuffed animals, and dolls with parts that could break off or be pulled off by little hands. Be alert to items that can choke children like balloons and plastic bags; keep them out of the infant and toddler areas.

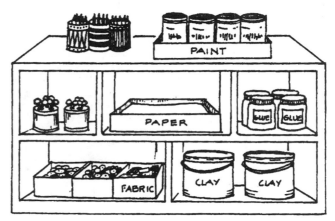

Select toys that are safe and appropriate for the age and developmental level of the children who use them. Be sure the toys are nontoxic and test all toys for durability and strength. Cloth toys should be made of flame resistant material. Inspect them frequently for damage where small pieces could easily be broken off. Keep wooden toys smooth and free from splinters. Check seams and decorations on cloth items for tearing and weak threads. Solicit the help of parents to maintain toys and mend broken ones. Store toys out of reach if they require adult supervision or if they have been mouthed by a child and not yet sanitized. Teach children how to play safely with all toys and equipment. Put the toys away after children have finished playing with them.

## *Outdoor Safety*

Outdoor time can be a time for children to experiment with different toys and materials. They can challenge themselves to try new physical skills like balancing, jumping, running, sliding, and riding. They can experiment with materials that can be used to build things.

An outdoor play area gives children the space they need to exercise their large muscles and attempt new skills without getting hurt. Caregivers must supervise the children closely at all times. However, the most vigilant caregiver will find it difficult to prevent injuries or accidents if the playground itself is hazardous. Outdoor play areas must be designed according to general safety criteria.

# CRITERIA FOR OUTSIDE SAFETY

- Set aside a separate play area for infants and toddlers, so that they can crawl and toddle without being bumped by older, more mobile children.

- Be sure that children do not use equipment in dangerous ways. Misusing equipment (walking up a slide) can cause injuries.

- Remove or fence off potentially hazardous or dangerous materials.

- Check play equipment and the environment daily. Look for sharp objects, rough surfaces, and loose or broken parts. Remove or repair unsafe equipment.

- Keep the area free from glass, litter, and large rocks.

- Cover playground surfaces with shock absorbing materials like sand, pea gravel, granulated wood chips, rubber matting, and shredded rubber.

- Prevent children from putting plants, grass, pebbles, or dirt into their mouths. Remove all outdoor plants that are toxic at any stage of growth.

- Do not use insecticides on plants and shrubs.

- Enclose the outdoor play space to keep the children from wandering away.

- Fence off water to prevent drownings. Children are fascinated by water and have no idea of its potential danger.

- Be vigilant. As children move about, they are hard to watch constantly and accidents happen quickly.

- Talk about safety often and model good safe practices for the children. Showing children how important their safety is to you is one more way of teaching them to value themselves and others.

A safe environment depends on caregivers and parents who are alert to potential hazards and the children at all times. By adhering to a schedule of periodic safety checks, repairing or removing dangerous items, and being safety conscious, the high-quality infant and toddler center maintains an environment that encourages children to explore and learn about their world.

## Emergency First Aid Procedures

All staff members should be trained in emergency first-aid procedures and cardiopulmonary resuscitation (CPR). This can make the difference between life and death.

No matter how safety-conscious the staff has been or how much planning has gone into developing careful and safe practices, emergencies will occur. Accidents will happen and they will happen suddenly. If comprehensive written emergency policies and procedures are in place and staff are trained, they will be prepared to handle such situations. The written policies should outline the roles and responsibilities of each staff member.

Procedures include something as simple as posting telephone numbers in the event of plumbing or electrical emergencies, injuries, illnesses, poisonings, fires, earthquakes, or severe weather emergencies. Parents should also have copies of the procedures so that they will know what to expect in an emergency and what is expected of them. In any emergency, follow these three basic rules:

---

### 1. *STAY CALM.*

### 2. *FOLLOW THE PROCEDURES.*

### 3. *ACT QUICKLY.*

---

Keep calm and do not panic. Your sympathetic kindness will nearly always soothe a child.

## Choking

All caregivers should know the proper techniques to help a choking child or infant. If a child has swallowed something and is coughing hard, let the child cough. Coughing is the body's way of getting rid of a foreign object in the throat or windpipe and becomes more effective when the child holds both arms straight up over his head. If the child cannot cough, talk, or breathe, use the following techniques:

---

### *WARNING:*
Use the following techniques only if the child can't cough, talk, or breathe.

---

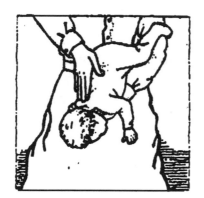 

---

### FOR A BABY UNDER ONE-YEAR OLD

• Hold the child in a jackknife position over your arm, with his head lower than his chest.

• With the palm of your hand give several quick blows to the child's back, between the shoulder blades.

• Repeat until the swallowed object breaks loose and comes out.

American Red Cross, 1993

---

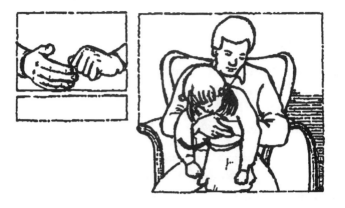

---

### FOR A TODDLER ONE YEAR OR OLDER USE
### THE HEIMLICH MANEUVER

- Stand behind the child and wrap your arms around the child's waist.

- Make a fist with one of your hands and grab it with the other hand.

- Place the fist against the child's stomach, just above the navel and below the rib cage.

- Press into the abdomen with a quick and upward thrust.

- Repeat at short intervals, until the object pops out and the child is breathing properly.

American Red Cross, 1993

---

*If these methods do not work, call an ambulance and continue these procedures until help comes. Do not stop trying.*

## Bumps and Bruises

Children have many minor accidents. Write down all facts and details about any accident on an Injury Report Form so that other caregivers and parents can watch for later symptoms. Showing concern will help the child feel better right away.

Cold compresses help stop pain and reduce swelling. An effective cold compress can be as simple as a washcloth dipped in cold water and wrung out, or ice cubes wrapped in a plastic bag or wash cloth.

Bumps to the head often look bad because they swell so much. Cold compresses relieve the swelling and pain of most head bumps. In the event of a hard blow to the head, notify the parents or get medical attention because it can cause a concussion. If any of the following symptoms are observed within three hours of any head injury, call for medical help immediately.

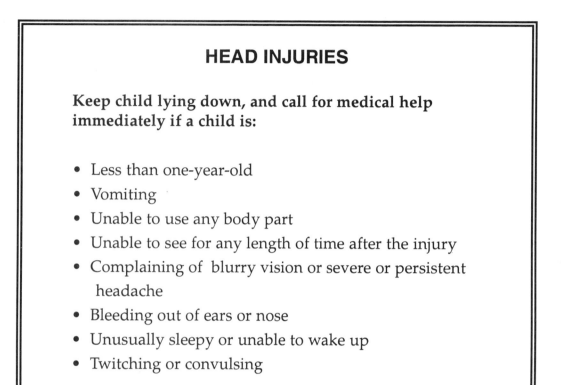

**HEAD INJURIES**

**Keep child lying down, and call for medical help immediately if a child is:**

- Less than one-year-old
- Vomiting
- Unable to use any body part
- Unable to see for any length of time after the injury
- Complaining of blurry vision or severe or persistent headache
- Bleeding out of ears or nose
- Unusually sleepy or unable to wake up
- Twitching or convulsing

## Burns

Burns are classified into three categories:

- *First-degree burns* are marked by redness or other skin discoloration, one or two small unbroken blisters, pain, and swelling. (An ordinary sunburn is typical of a first-degree burn.) Run cold water over the burn for five minutes or more. You may also cover the burn with a cold wet washcloth or ice pack. Be careful not to break blisters.

- *Second-degree burns* are often the result of exposure to flame, scalding liquids, or a very severe sunburn. The skin is usually reddish, mottled, and damaged, with blisters and signs of body fluid loss. These burns require immediate professional medical care. While waiting, run cold water over the burn for five minutes or more. You may also cover the burn with a cold, wet washcloth or ice pack.

- *Third-degree burns* are marked by damage to tissues beneath the skin. The area may resemble a second-degree burn at first, but progresses to a whitish or charred coloration. Third-degree burns often result from contact with high-voltage electricity, steam, or boiling water, or from an accident in which the person is trapped in burning clothing. Call for medical help immediately. If possible, gently spray cool water from a hose or shower on the covered burn while waiting for help. *Nothing should be applied to a third-degree burn. Do not even remove clothing from burn areas because the skin may come off with the fabric.* However, burn areas can be covered temporarily with sterile gauze pads, clean sheets, or a sterilized wet cloth.

  If the third-degree burn victim is conscious and not vomiting, offer small amounts of lukewarm water containing a teaspoon of salt and one-half teaspoon of baking soda per quart of liquid, sipped at a rate of one ounce every four or five minutes.

*NEVER apply ointments or grease (including butter or margarine), baking soda, or other household substances to a burned skin area.*

## Nosebleeds

Nosebleeds are usually caused by allergies, colds, or dried-out membranes in the nose. They are almost never serious, but the sight of blood can frighten a child. The best way to treat a nosebleed is to have the child sit down and lean his body forward. Firmly pinch the child's nostrils together with a cold, damp washcloth or paper towel until the bleeding stops. Make the child stay still and quiet to prevent the bleeding from starting again. If the bleeding won't stop, contact the parents or medical personnel.

## Object in Ear or Nose

Young children sometimes put objects in their noses and ears and are unable to remove them. Do not prod anything out unless you can easily see it; you could push it in further. Contact health personnel to get instruction.

## Poisoning

Many substances are poisonous to children. All cleaning supplies and medications should be kept out of children's reach; lock medications in a safe place. Other potentially poisonous substances are often overlooked. For example, some art materials are toxic to infants and toddlers. Use only those that are labeled "non-toxic" and watch the children closely to keep them from mouthing brushes, crayons, or paints. Infants are at risk of poisoning if they swallow or inhale certain lotions or talcum powders. Caregivers must be especially careful when changing diapers to be sure that the infant does not mouth a container and swallow some of the contents.

Young children are attracted to plants and flowers that can be deadly if swallowed. It is best to keep all indoor plants out of their reach. Staff should learn which plants are poisonous and remove them. Supervise young children closely around outdoor plants.

Teach children never to put plants, fruits, or berries in their mouth unless an adult has offered them to the child. If a caregiver believes a child has swallowed something poisonous, she should follow these procedures immediately, before the poison can take effect:

## WHAT TO DO IN CASE OF POISONING

- Immediately call the local poison control center, hospital emergency room, or physician.

- Call parents.

- Try to find out exactly what the child swallowed. Find the container the poisonous substance came from or a leaf of a plant that the child ate.

- Follow the instructions from the poison control center very carefully.
    - √ You might be directed to make the child drink milk or water to dilute the poison.
    - √ You might have to induce vomiting by using syrup of ipecac or using another method.

- If the child vomits, save a sample of the vomit.

- Some poisons have delayed effects. Ask whether the child will need to be observed afterward and for how long. Make sure the child's parents understand the instructions.

*Do not induce vomiting unless the directions specifically tell you to do so. Some poisons are corrosive and vomiting them back up can cause even more damage to the child's throat and esophagus.*

## First Aid Kits

Each classroom should have a complete first aid kit, accessible to staff at all times but out of reach of children.

---

### CONTENTS OF A FIRST AID KIT

A first aid kit should contain at least the following items:

- Disposable nonporous gloves
- Sealed packages of alcohol wipes or antiseptic
- Scissors
- Tweezers
- Thermometer
- Bandage tape
- Sterile gauze pads
- Flexible roller gauze
- Triangular bandages
- Safety pins
- Eye dressing
- Syrup of ipecac
- Cold pack
- Red Cross standard first aid text or equivalent first aid guide
- Insect sting preparation
- Hospital or poison control center telephone number
- Small plastic or metal splints
- Pencil and notepad
- Sealable plastic bag for soiled materials

---

## *Emergency Precautions*

### Fire

Safe exits should be clearly marked and plans established for alternate routes of escape. Hold unannounced "fire drills" *at least* twice a year. Evacuate the building as soon as the fire alarm sounds or smoke or fire is visible. Move quickly because fire spreads rapidly and seconds truly count. Carry infants or push them in a crib. Walk with or carry toddlers. One person should be responsible for checking all out-of-the-way or seldom-used places like bathrooms, hallways, and closets to be sure that no one is trapped or overcome by smoke. Proceed directly to a designated area away from the building to get the children out of harm's way. Take attendance immediately to account for all children and adults. Do not go back into the building until the firefighters say it is safe.

## Severe Weather Emergencies

Have some communication system available (radio or television) which will keep staff aware of the current status of storms. During storms, keep everyone away from glass mirrors and windows that may shatter due to high winds or falling objects. Keep children protected and close to the caregivers. Teach older toddlers how to "duck and cover." If inside a building, this means getting under a table or in a doorway, and away from windows. Have the children protect their heads and bodies from any flying debris in the event of strong winds or earthquakes. Take attendance of all children and adults immediately.

## Emergency Kits

Assemble and store an emergency kit where it is likely to be accessible but undamaged in the event of a severe storm or earthquake. Use the list below to assemble a supply kit for emergency situations.

---

### SUPPLY KIT FOR EMERGENCY SITUATIONS

- Battery-powered radio
- Heavy-duty flashlights and batteries
- Canned or packaged food
- Bottled water
- First aid supplies
- Diapers
- Anti-bacterial baby wipes

---

# Checklist for a Safe Environment

Use these questions as guides to design and maintain a safe environment for infants and toddlers.

√ Are electrical outlets covered?

√ Are all electrical cords out of the reach of children?

√ Are materials to be used by infants and toddlers non-toxic?

√ Is the floor covered with non-skid rugs or well-padded flooring to prevent accidents?

√ Are non-breakable toys and materials used in the classroom and in the outdoor play area?

√ Are checks for broken toys made routinely?

√ Does all equipment meet safety guidelines (secure, no sharp corners, no small parts, etc.)?

√ Does furniture have rounded corners? If not, are sharp corners covered with soft covering?

√ Are windows and mirrors made of shatter-proof glass?

√ Are toys and materials within easy reach of children to inhibit climbing in unsafe areas?

√ Are storage shelves placed away from windows and securely anchored to the wall?

√ Is there adequate space for children to move freely?

√ Are fabrics, including curtains, made of non-flammable fabric?

√ Are carpets and equipment easy to clean?

√ Are cleaning materials, medications, and other hazardous items stored in locked areas with no access by young children?

√ Are climbing areas provided with cushions for falling?

√ Are trash cans covered and out of reach of infants and toddlers?

√ Are safety guards placed on hot water faucets to prevent young children from burning themselves?

√ Is there a safe crawling area for infants and young children?

√ Are gates installed to prevent children from moving to dangerous places (e.g., at stairs, doors)?

√ Are all plastic bags out of reach of the infants and toddlers?

√ Are all plants kept out of the reach of children?

√ Are written procedures for accidents and weather emergencies posted prominently and made available to staff and parents?

√ Are emergency numbers posted next to the telephones?

√ Are first-aid supplies readily available?

√ Is there adequate storage for toys and materials?

√ Are staff trained in first aid techniques for burns, choking, bruises, nosebleeds, poisoning, etc.?

√ Are outdoor areas fenced and free of glass and litter?

# CHAPTER 14

# PROMOTING GOOD NUTRITION

# 14. PROMOTING GOOD NUTRITION

The medical research cited in Chapter 2 confirms that a mother's balanced, nutritious diet during pregnancy has positive and lasting effects on the development of the fetus, particularly the development of the brain. Moreover, a balanced, nutritious diet is crucial to children's cognitive development after birth and is essential to their continuing physical health and growth. This chapter discusses the importance of the mealtime environment, the changes in children's dietary needs as they grow, and the importance of communicating with parents about food.

## The Importance of Mealtimes

Obviously, mealtimes are important for children's nutrition; they are social and learning times as well. Caregivers who plan pleasant, nutritious meals help babies develop solid, lifelong eating habits. They adjust meal and snack menus and schedule feeding times to meet the different needs of infants and toddlers. Young infants eat on demand, satisfying their ravenous appetites, while older infants and toddlers require small amounts of food, served frequently. Children should be encouraged, but not forced, to eat.

Meal and snack schedules and weekly menus should be posted on the Parents' Bulletin Board. Each family should receive a copy of the weekly menu and receive the *What I Did Today* form or *Daily Information Sheet* (Chapter 11) that informs parents about what and how much their child eats each day.

Feeding times should be pleasant social and learning experiences for the infants and toddlers. Hold infants and talk to them when feeding them with a bottle. For older infants and toddlers, at least one adult should sit with the children to help them eat, demonstrate good manners, and encourage conversation, especially while they are waiting to be served. Serve meals in a family-style group, with each child served individually.

Chairs, tables, and eating utensils should be suitable for the size and developmental levels of the children. Various foods can broaden the children's food experiences and accommodate ethnic and cultural preferences. Schedule sufficient time for children to eat—do not rush them. Never use food as a punishment or reward.

The eating and feeding area should be a cheerful area with easy-to-clean surfaces and child-sized furniture. Very young infants should be held by the caregiver and fed one at a time. Older infants can use chairs that clip onto the tables or special child-sized feeding chairs. Mobile infants can use regular child-sized tables and chairs. Their feet should touch the ground when they are seated and the table should be below chest level. Toddlers will enjoy sitting in groups of two to four at small tables.

Managing the multiple demands of mealtime is a complicated task—to provide healthy, nutritious food on time to hungry children, help them eat, monitor who is eating what, and make meals pleasant events for caregivers and children. Chapter 9 and Chapter 15, *Physical Space: Designing Responsive Environments for Infants and Toddlers,* provide additional information on mealtime settings and routines.

## *The Changing Dietary Needs of Growing Children*

Children's nutritional needs change dramatically between birth and three years and the infant and toddler program must accommodate these differences.

The child who eats regular, nutritious meals and snacks is likely be healthier and less susceptible to disease than a child whose diet is not adequate to his needs. During the first year of life a newborn baby triples in weight and increases in length approximately one and a half times; her nutritional needs are more critical to future health and well-being than at any other time of life. Feeding times are important events in a baby's life because hunger comes often and intensely when the body demands fuel. Feeding not only satisfies the physical demand but also tells the baby that her environment is responsive to her needs. Satisfying a baby's nutritional needs lays the foundation for later physical health and cognitive ability.

### Young Infants

Young infants' nutritional needs are satisfied by a milk diet, either breast or bottled. Breast-feeding is one of nature's ideal systems. Breast milk is the best possible food for a baby, providing all that he needs to thrive and grow for the first months of life. Breast milk contains natural antibodies that strengthen the infant's immune system. It is economical and hygienic because there are no bottles and nipples to sterilize and no water to boil. Furthermore, breast-feeding also meets a new mother's emotional and social needs as it reinforces the close, intimate relationship between mother and baby. Because breast-feeding has so many benefits, caregivers should encourage mothers to nurse their infants and provide emotional and practical support for those who do.

---

### PROCEDURES FOR THE SAFE STORAGE OF BREAST MILK

- Refrigerate breast milk as soon as possible.
- Store breast milk in single-feeding sterilized bottles.
- Store breast milk in the refrigerator for a maximum of 48 hours. Do not use it after 48 hours.
- Breast milk can be kept frozen for a maximum of two weeks from the time it is pumped and frozen.
- Thaw frozen breast milk in the refrigerator or under cold running water, not in a microwave.
- Shake the bottle of thawed milk gently to mix.
- Dispose of unused milk immediately after the infant finishes feeding.
- Do not refreeze thawed breast milk.

---

The length of time that a baby stays at the breast for a feeding varies. Most newborns will nurse for at least 15 minutes, and finish in less than an hour. Have a comfortable chair in a restful, quiet place for the mother and child.

Many women continue to breast-feed their babies after returning to work by pumping breast milk into a bottle for the baby. For such arrangements, follow the procedures on the previous page to keep the milk safe and the baby happy!

The American Academy of Pediatrics advises using only breast milk or iron-fortified infant formula during the first year of life. Cow's milk (whole milk, not skim or lowfat milk) can be introduced between six and 12 months of age.

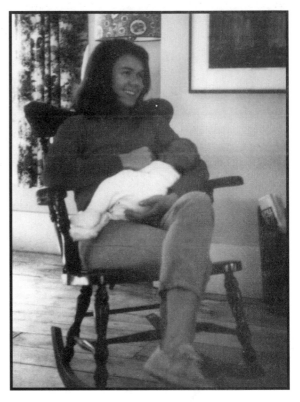

Weaning is an individual decision. The baby's adjustment is eased when weaning is done gradually and patiently. When the mother decides to wean, it is important that she and the caregiver gradually offer more liquids in a cup or bottle at mealtimes and between meals. Nursing as well as bottle feedings before naps should gradually be replaced by other soothing and relaxing activities such as soft music or a back rub.

## Older Infants

Pediatricians recommend starting solid food when infants are between four and six months of age by gradually introducing cereals. Allow time for the baby to become accustomed to each new food. Because the infant's neuromuscular skills are not well developed, solid foods must be introduced carefully. Add soft, pureed vegetables and

fruits to the child's diet between six and eight months. Use caution when introducing solids and finger foods. Avoid nuts, small bits of carrots, and small pieces of hard fruits until the child can easily chew and swallow them. Between eight and nine months, the child can be offered food with lumps that can easily be chewed, mashed, or swallowed whole. By the end of the first year, the baby should be able to eat most table foods.

## FEEDING TIPS FOR INFANTS

- Every baby is different!
- Do not feel pressured to start a baby eating solid foods too soon. (A baby's digestive system is not sufficiently developed to digest solid food until four to six months of age.)
- Do not put a baby to bed with a bottle. This can cause ear infections and tooth decay.
- Add one new food at a time. Wait approximately five days before introducing another food.
- Use whole milk. Skim or lowfat milk does not have the fat that the brain and nerves need to grow during the early years.
- Use fresh, cooked foods.
- Do not add sugar, butter, or salt to young children's food.

## Toddlers

The nutritional needs of infants and toddlers differ by amount, frequency of feeding, and type of food. Because toddlers' growth rate is slower than that of infants, toddlers eat relatively smaller amounts and they eat less frequently. They also may begin to take more control over the type and amount of food they eat. During this stage, toddlers may eat only a few foods and reject many others.

A variety of acceptable foods encourages children to select what they want to eat. If a variety of nutritional foods is available, most toddlers will be well-nourished. Children between one to three years of age consume approximately 1000 to 1300 calories per day.

Serve small portions and encourage toddlers to try at least one bite of each food. Toddlers should use child-sized eating utensils, but will also investigate their food by touching and smelling. A choice of foods, a chance to eat some food with their hands and other food with their own utensils, and plenty of time to enjoy the social aspects of mealtimes will encourage the child to become independent and feel he has some control in an important area of his life. Helping toddlers to develop healthy attitudes about food is important for good health.

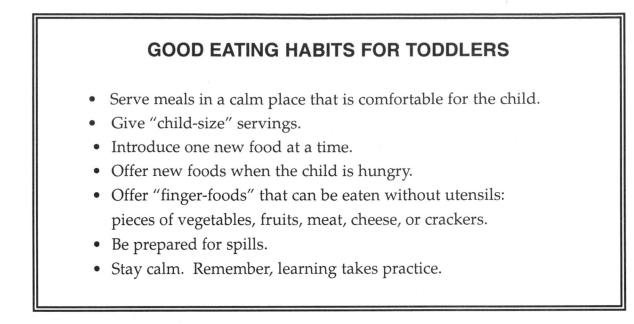

**GOOD EATING HABITS FOR TODDLERS**

- Serve meals in a calm place that is comfortable for the child.
- Give "child-size" servings.
- Introduce one new food at a time.
- Offer new foods when the child is hungry.
- Offer "finger-foods" that can be eaten without utensils: pieces of vegetables, fruits, meat, cheese, or crackers.
- Be prepared for spills.
- Stay calm. Remember, learning takes practice.

## *Communicating With Parents*

It is extremely important that parents and caregivers keep each other informed about a child's eating habits. Any recurring eating problem should be discussed with the child's parents. (See Chapters 10 and 11.)

Parent meetings should offer information about nutrition and healthy eating habits. At these meetings, ask parent volunteers to visit the classroom and prepare special foods with the children.

The following suggestions for a healthy diet, provided by the United States Department of Agriculture and the Department of Health and Human Services, will be helpful in discussing ways to promote good nutrition for children.

## Suggestions for Healthy Eating Habits

- Eat a variety of foods.
- After age two, avoid more than moderate portions of foods high in saturated fat and cholesterol: fatty meats, butter, cream, lard, shortenings, and goods containing palm or coconut oils.

  √ Use skim or lowfat milk and milk products. (*Whole milk is important before age two.*)
  √ Choose lean meat (trim off fat), fish, poultry, and dried beans as sources of protein.
  √ Broil, bake, or boil, rather than fry, foods.

- Choose foods high in fiber and starch, such as whole grain beads and cereals, fruits and vegetables, and dried beans and peas.
- Avoid foods high in salt.
- Avoid foods high in sugar.

## *Conclusion*

Good nutrition is an investment in the future. As children learn about good nutrition, they will begin to acquire healthy, lifelong eating habits. When meals are pleasant and nutritious, and food choices are coordinated with parents, children's healthy development is assured.

## GUIDELINES FOR A HEALTHY DIET FOR INFANTS*

| Age of Baby | Breakfast | Lunch | Snack |
|---|---|---|---|
| Birth through 3 months | 4-6 fl. oz. breast milk or formula | 4-6 fl. oz. breast milk or formula | 4-6 fl. oz. breast milk or formula |
| 4 months through 7 months | 4-8 fl. oz. breast milk or formula<br><br>0-3 tablespoons infant cereal (optional) | 4-8 fl. oz. breast milk or formula<br><br>0-3 tablespoons infant cereal (optional)<br><br>0-3 tablespoons fruit and/or vegetable (optional) | 4-6 fl. oz. breast milk or formula |
| 8 months through 11 months | 6-8 fl. oz. breast milk, formula, or whole milk | 6-8 fl. oz. breast milk, formula, or whole milk<br><br>3 tbsp. meat, fish, poultry, egg yolk, or cooked dry beans or peas, or 1-4 oz. cottage cheese, cheese food, or 1/2 to 2 oz. cheese<br><br>1-4 tbsp. fruit or vegetable | 2-fl. oz. breast-milk, formula, whole milk, or fruit juice (optional) |

*Conversion tables for the amounts served can be found in Appendix B.

## GUIDELINES FOR A HEALTHY DIET FOR TODDLERS*

| Food Groups | Servings Per Day | Serving Sizes |
|---|---|---|
| Milk and Milk Products<br>Note: Lowfat and skim milk should not be given before 2 years of age. | 3 (18-24 oz.) | 3/4 to 1 cup milk<br>or 3/4 cup plain yogurt |
| Meat or Meat Alternative | 2 | 1 oz. meat, fish or poultry<br>or 1/2 cup peas or beans<br>or 2 tbsp. peanut butter |
| Vegetables and Fruit | 4 (for Vitamin A) | 1/8 to 1/4 cup of carrots, sweet potatoes, squash, broccoli, or cantaloupe |
| Vegetables and Fruit | 10 (for Vitamin C) | 1/2 cup or 1 small piece oranges, strawberries, grapefruit, orange or grapefruit juice, green peppers, broccoli |
|  | Other vitamins and minerals | 1/4 cup or 1 small piece potatoes, corn, green beans, peas, lettuce, cabbage, cucumbers, tomatoes, apples, bananas, grapes, plums, apricots |
| Breads and Cereals | 4 | 1/2 slice of bread<br>1/4 cup rice, macaroni, or dry cereal or 1 to 2 tbs. hot cereal |
| Fats, oils, and sugar | **Use limited amounts.** These foods are high in calories, sugar, fat and/or salt. | Margarine, butter, vegetable oils, lard, mayonnaise, salad dressing, bacon, sausage, candy, cookies, chips, soda pop |

*Conversion tables for the amounts served can be found in Appendix B.

# Kinds and Amounts of Foods to Be Served to Meet
# 1/2 of Daily Nutritional Needs of Children

**SIZE PER SERVING**

| Food Group | 1 to 3 Years | 4 to 6 Years | 7 and Older |
|---|---|---|---|
| **1. Milk or Milk Products** | | | |
| Milk | 1 $1/2$ cups | 1 $1/2$ cups | 1 $1/2$ cups |
| or Cheese | 1 $1/4$ cups | 1 $1/2$ cups | 2 cups |
| or Dried Milk | 4 tablespoons | 4 tablespoons | 4 tablespoons |

Other servings which equal $1/2$ cup of milk: $1/2$ cup yogurt or 1 cup cottage cheese

| | | | |
|---|---|---|---|
| **2. Meat and Meat Alternates** | | | |
| Meat, Fish, Poultry (cooked) | 1 ounce | 1 $1/2$ ounces | 2 ounces |
| or Egg | $1/2$ egg | 1 egg | 1 egg |
| or Peanut Butter | 1 tablespoon | 1 $1/2$ tablespoons | 2 tablespoons |
| or Cooked Dried Beans or Peas | $1/4$ cup | $3/8$ cup | 1 cup |
| Cheese | 1 ounce | 2 ounces | 3 ounces |

| | | | |
|---|---|---|---|
| **3. Vegetable Group** | $1/4$ cup | $1/2$ cup | $3/4$ cup |

| | | | |
|---|---|---|---|
| **4. Fruit Group** | $1/4$ cup or $1/2$ cup juice | $1/2$ cup or 1 cup juice | $3/4$ cup or 1 $1/2$ cups juice |

Vitamin C Source Daily and Vitamin A Source 3 times weekly

| | | | |
|---|---|---|---|
| **5. Breads and Cereals\*** | | | |
| Sliced Bread | 2 slices | 2 slices | 2 slices |
| or Dry Cereal | $3/4$ cup | 1 cup | $1^1/4$ cup |
| or Cooked Cereal | $3/4$ cup | 1 cup | $1^1/4$ cup |
| or Rice or Noodles | 1 cup | $1^1/4$ cup | 1 $1/4$ cup |

\*Whole Grain or Enriched

Source: Texas Department of Regulatory Services. (1995). *Day-care center minimum standards and guide-lines.* Austin, TX: author.

# CHAPTER 15

# PHYSICAL SPACE: DESIGNING RESPONSIVE ENVIRONMENTS FOR INFANTS AND TODDLERS

# 15. PHYSICAL SPACE: DESIGNING RESPONSIVE ENVIRONMENTS FOR INFANTS AND TODDLERS

The environment itself is a valuable teacher for infants and toddlers. Young children use all of their senses as they learn and develop; therefore, all aspects of their surroundings affect the information and messages they receive.

This chapter considers how to organize space and equipment to support and promote the developmental needs of infants and toddlers in a comfortable and inviting environment.

Both the physical climate and the emotional climate must be considered when designing space for very young children. First, the physical space itself should be organized to meet children's needs to play, eat, sleep, crawl, walk, sit, cuddle, and be toileted. Second, the physical surroundings should be set up so that staff can easily respond to the emotional, social, cognitive, and physical needs of the young children in their care. Young children need group and private time, cuddle time and independent time, and time for quiet and noisy activities.

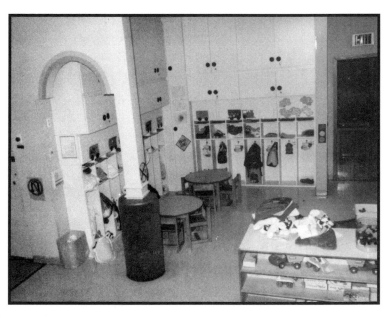

## The Physical Climate

Young children grow, develop, and learn best when they are comfortable. Temperature, lighting, moisture, and noise levels all affect children's comfort.

## Temperature

The environment should be neither too warm nor too cold, particularly at floor level, where infants and toddlers spend most of their time. A moderately low heat setting is recommended. Children who are too warm frequently become lethargic or sleepy, and are less likely to interact with their surroundings. At the same time, floors should not be cold or drafty.

Let in fresh air as much as possible. If fans are used, be sure that the cords and blades are inaccessible to children. The flow of air should be even.

## Lighting

Lighting needs vary by activity. The napping areas should be dim, yet still allow caregivers to monitor sleeping children. Play areas should be well lit. Natural light is pleasant for young children. Indoor lighting can include both fluorescent and incandescent lights. Outdoor play space should include sunny and shady areas.

## Moisture

In areas of high humidity or heavy rains, it is important to minimize moisture, a favorite environment of molds and bacteria. Dehumidifiers may be used to remove excess moisture from the air. Rugs must be kept dry at all times. In dry, arid areas, humidifiers may be necessary to restore moisture balance in the classroom.

## Noise Levels

There should be adequate space between noisy and quiet areas so that the needs of infants and toddlers in each area can be met. Noise levels should be kept low in the children's sleeping areas. Active areas, which are noisier, should be away from sleeping areas. If noise is a problem because of the room's acoustics, the walls may be covered with carpeting to reduce the sound level. It is important to remember that active toddlers will be noisy, but even very young children can learn rules about quiet times and areas. Consider the following checklist when designing child care space for infants and toddlers.

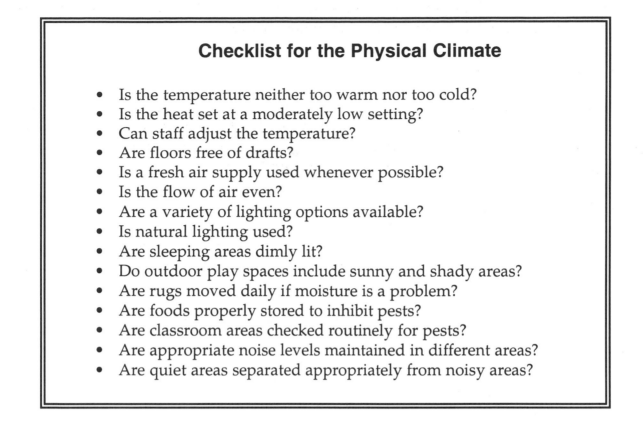

**Checklist for the Physical Climate**

- Is the temperature neither too warm nor too cold?
- Is the heat set at a moderately low setting?
- Can staff adjust the temperature?
- Are floors free of drafts?
- Is a fresh air supply used whenever possible?
- Is the flow of air even?
- Are a variety of lighting options available?
- Is natural lighting used?
- Are sleeping areas dimly lit?
- Do outdoor play spaces include sunny and shady areas?
- Are rugs moved daily if moisture is a problem?
- Are foods properly stored to inhibit pests?
- Are classroom areas checked routinely for pests?
- Are appropriate noise levels maintained in different areas?
- Are quiet areas separated appropriately from noisy areas?

## *The Emotional and Developmental Climate*

Just as the physical environment is important to the well-being of infants and toddlers, so is a climate that supports and encourages their emotional and developmental growth. Here again, the childcare environment must be planned carefully. The environment must be cheerful and inviting; it must be adequate for solitary play, play with or next to peers, play with the caregiving adults, and quiet time alone with an adult. Carpeted floors keep the space warmer, decrease noise, and make a safer, more comfortable place for children to play and teachers to sit.

Children need choices of "private places" as well as "playful places." Infants and toddlers need adequate space in order to move and explore their environments. Generally, the recommended guideline is 30 to 50 square feet of space for each infant and toddler. However, *how* the space is used and *how* the room is arranged is as important as the amount of space available.

## Choices

The physical environment should offer choices to the infants and toddlers. Choices are encouraged when materials are easily accessible so that the children can reach them, and when the environment offers a variety of options for play. An open center of the classroom allows children to see the different choices they have. The preferences of infants differ from those of toddlers, and the environment should provide choices that reflect those differences. When choices are offered and encouraged by their caregivers, young children understand that their increasing independence is valued.

## Private Places and Playful Spaces

From time to time, all children want to be by themselves. A chance to be alone is especially important for children who are in the classroom for the entire day. Children should have access to solitary areas in the classroom away from noisy activities. The private area may include a beanbag chair, a loft, or a child-size rocking chair.

Other areas should be designed for high levels of movement as well as activities with less movement. Infants should have their own open areas, safe for crawling, apart from older children.

## An Inviting Environment

An interesting and colorful environment "invites" children to explore, investigate, and play.  Bright colorful pictures, posters, photographs, and children's art should be hung at the children's eye level.

## Toys, Materials, and Equipment

A variety of interesting toys and materials suitable for infants and toddlers should be available and accessible to the children, so they can make their own choices.  The materials should encourage children to use their vision, hearing, smell, and touch as they interact with them.  They should be easy to clean.  It is preferable to have duplicate toys available so that infants and toddlers are not expected to wait for materials.  Children of this age have not yet learned the social skill of sharing and often the most popular toy is the one with no duplicate in the center!

Each infant and toddler should have her own cot or crib.  This is important not only for reasons of hygiene, but also because it provides the child with consistency and routine that contribute to the development of a sense of self.

Child-sized tables and chairs, rocking chairs, and couches are easier and safer for children to use, take up less space, and contribute to the sense that "this is my place." Shelves for the toys should be at a toddler's eye level.  Adult rocking chairs should be available so that caregivers can soothe infants and toddlers who are upset, tired, hurt, not feeling well, or being read or sung to.

The carefully planned childcare environment supports and encourages learning and development.  Safe, clean environments that incorporate child-friendly materials and equipment and include areas dedicated to a variety of specific activities encourage the active exploration and development that will best serve the children.

*Checklist for the Emotional and Developmental Climate* suggests questions to be considered when designing environments that will promote healthy emotional and developmental growth of infants and toddlers.

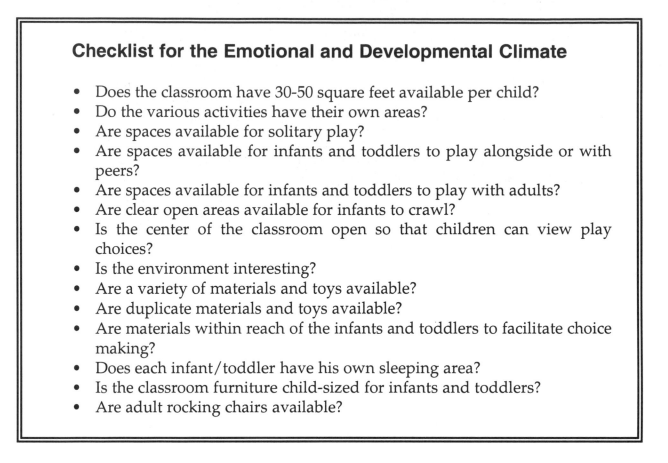

**Checklist for the Emotional and Developmental Climate**

- Does the classroom have 30-50 square feet available per child?
- Do the various activities have their own areas?
- Are spaces available for solitary play?
- Are spaces available for infants and toddlers to play alongside or with peers?
- Are spaces available for infants and toddlers to play with adults?
- Are clear open areas available for infants to crawl?
- Is the center of the classroom open so that children can view play choices?
- Is the environment interesting?
- Are a variety of materials and toys available?
- Are duplicate materials and toys available?
- Are materials within reach of the infants and toddlers to facilitate choice making?
- Does each infant/toddler have his own sleeping area?
- Is the classroom furniture child-sized for infants and toddlers?
- Are adult rocking chairs available?

## *Outdoor Spaces*

Most children love to be outdoors. Although the environment is less restrictive and activities tend to be more spontaneous, outdoor spaces can have enormous learning value if they are carefully planned. Unlike the fixed indoor environment, the outdoors is forever changing. Light, sounds, smells, temperature, and sensations of wind, rain, cold, and humidity yield opportunities for infants and toddlers to learn.

Just as with indoor areas, outdoor play areas call for sufficient space for movement, separated play areas for infants and toddlers, sunny and shady places, noisy and quiet activity areas, soft ground surfaces, adequate storage space, and an ample supply of outdoor materials. Staff must be alert to the health and safety requirements of outdoor spaces addressed in Chapters 12 and 13.

## Opportunities for Learning

The outdoor play area provides rich opportunities for social, emotional, language, cognitive, and physical learning.

***Social Development*** Even at this age children begin to negotiate for bikes and equipment they want to play with. They learn self-help skills by getting onto a swing, or gathering the pails and shovels they need. They exercise choice and independence when deciding whether to visit the rabbit or play in the sand.

***Emotional Development*** A child's self-confidence and trust in adults is reinforced when she is encouraged to take appropriate risks within the secure range of her caregiver. That first slide ride will probably elicit louder squeals of pride and delight than comparable indoor successes.

***Language Development*** The outdoor environment offers almost endless things to talk about, from butterflies to baby's busy feet. Toddlers love to chant rhythmically as they swing or see-saw.

***Cognitive Development*** Much of the knowledge acquired by infants and toddlers comes very naturally from their outdoor experiences. Sensory concepts, cause and effect relationships, colors, and shapes, to name a few, are informally taught in the outdoor setting.

***Physical Development*** Strength, coordination, balance, and stamina develop through freedom of movement and endless practice outdoors.

Outdoor play provides a change of scene. Take stuffed animals and toys outside onto a blanket. Plan feeding time or snack time outdoors for a change. Carry water in containers to the sand box and see what happens. Listen to the wind chimes. Watch the birds nest. Feel the snow fall. Finger paint. Relax with the children and share the fun as they learn.

## Outdoor Equipment and Materials

The outdoor play area should contain riding and climbing equipment, a sand box, and swings. The riding areas must be separated from other areas. Climbing equipment and swings should be surrounded by a four-inch layer of soft material such as sand or mulch. Outdoor materials include pails, shovels, balls, and riding toys. All outdoor play equipment should be specifically designed for infants and toddlers.

Infants and toddlers should play outdoors at least once daily and preferably twice. As often as possible, caregivers should take them beyond the confines of the playground. Walks in the park, to the zoo, and within the neighborhood expand children's perspective and enrich the context of their daily activities.

Family members are usually willing to assist with outdoor care and activities. Those who are ill at ease in the classroom are often eager to help outside. Be sure family members know the safety procedures for the outdoor environment.

*Checklist for Outdoor Space* suggests questions to consider when planning the outdoor playground for infants and toddlers.

---

## Checklist for Outdoor Space

- Is adequate space available for outdoor play?
- Are sunny and shady places available?
- Are infant and toddler areas separate?
- Are both noisy and quiet play spaces available?
- Are spaces available for both high and low movement activities?
- Is there adequate storage space for equipment and materials?
- Are activity areas clearly marked?
- Are riding areas separate from other play areas?
- Are children visible in all areas of the outdoor space?
- Are climbing structures available to encourage gross motor activities?
- Is outdoor play equipment specifically designed for infants and toddlers?
- Is a variety of toys available?
- Is 4-6 inches of ground covering used to cushion falls?
- Is the sand checked regularly to ensure adequate amounts?

---

## *A Final Note*

An environment that is comfortable and inviting is as important as one that is safe and healthy. It helps to minimize negative behavior, and it facilitates joyful learning.

# A WELL-PLANNED ROOM FOR YOUNG INFANTS

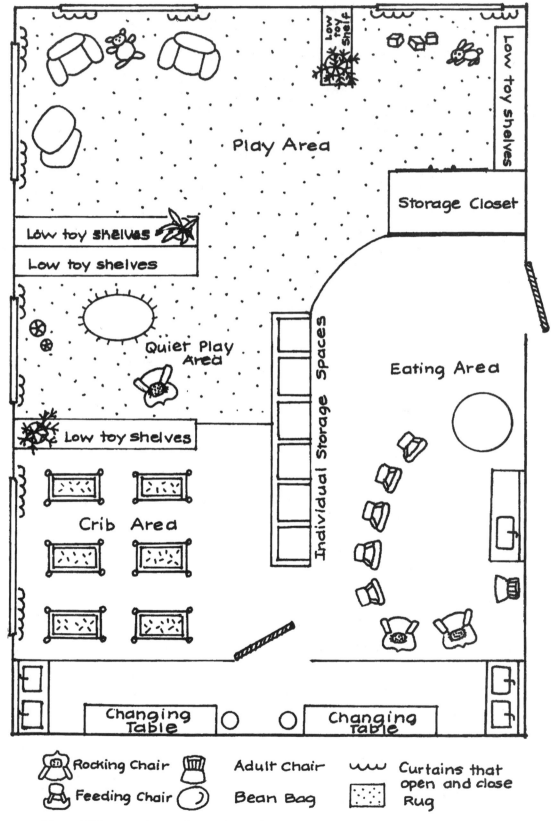

Note: This room is not drawn to scale.

## A WELL-PLANNED ROOM FOR MOBILE INFANTS

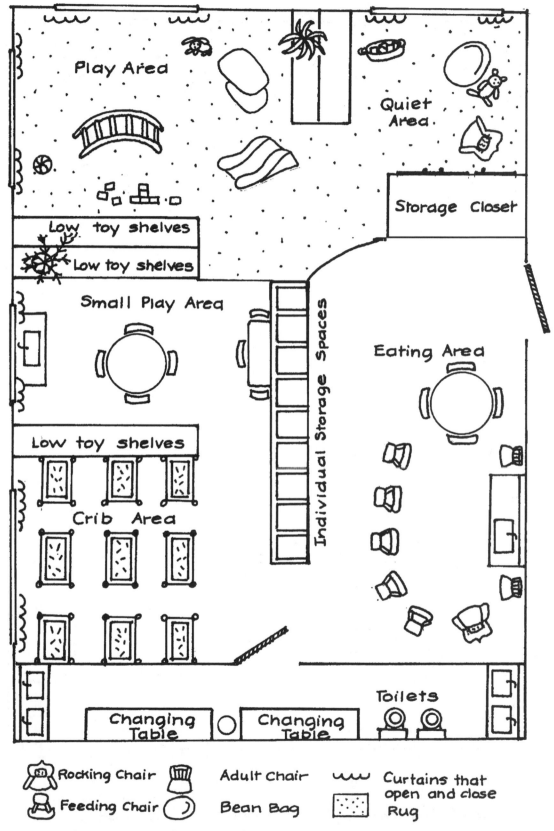

Note: This room is not drawn to scale.

## A WELL-PLANNED ROOM FOR TODDLERS

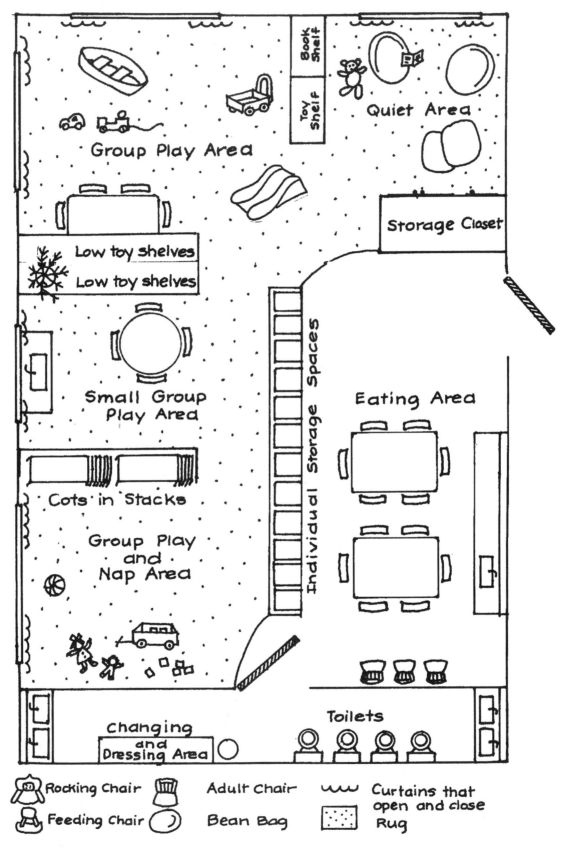

Note: This room is not drawn to scale.

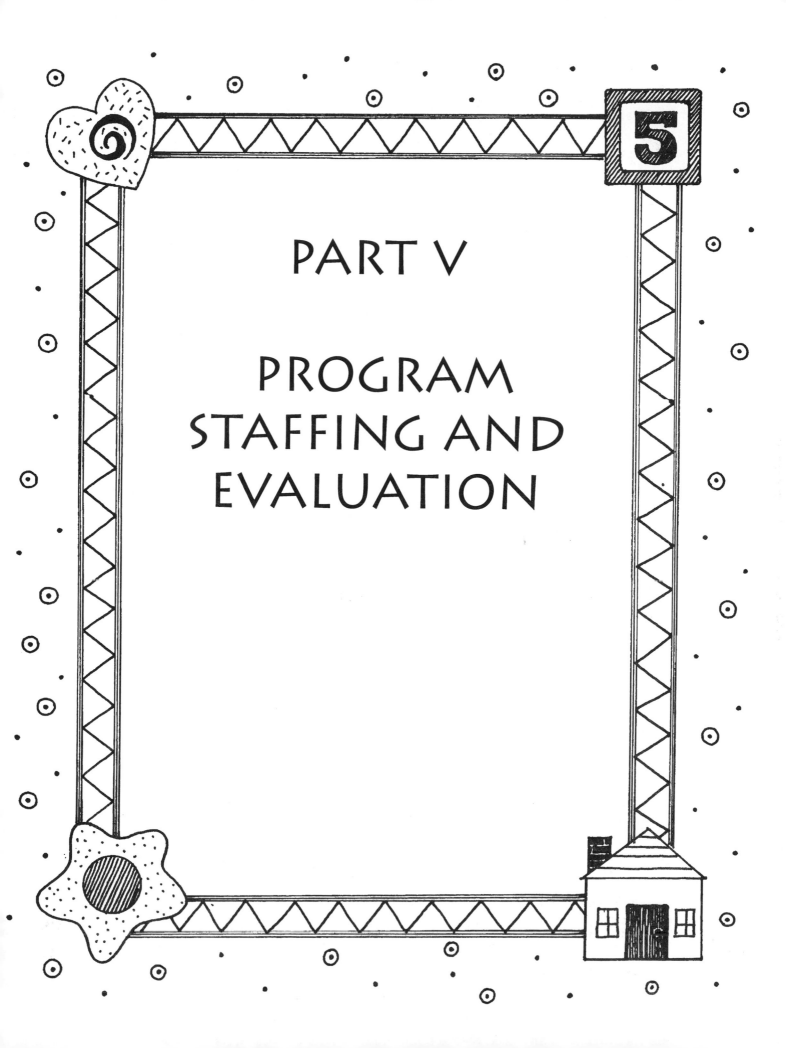

PART V

PROGRAM
STAFFING AND
EVALUATION

# CHAPTER 16

# STAFFING AND EVALUATING INFANT AND TODDLER PROGRAMS

# 16. STAFFING AND EVALUATING INFANT AND TODDLER PROGRAMS

This manual has discussed best practice in working with infants and toddlers, including the research base supporting that practice. In order to assure the application of best practice to the practical world of infant and toddler care and education, administrative issues must be addressed. Although many factors contribute to well administered programs, the heart of a quality program for infants and toddlers is the staff. Caring adults who are knowledgeable about child development, accepting of differences, and who are happy in the daily company of infants and toddlers are critical to a successful program. This chapter discusses essential staffing issues: staff selection, child/staff ratios, group size, continuity of care, staff training and education, guidance from supervisory staff, and staff and program evaluation.

## Staff Selection

The staff who work with very young children, especially the primary caregivers, must love children and want to be around them. Teaching the very young is an extremely demanding profession—physically, emotionally, and intellectually. Not everyone has the ability to sustain an enriching experience for infants and toddlers. No amount of educational preparation or training can supplement a caregiver who does not enjoy being with children.

Those caregivers who truly enjoy their jobs are more inclined to be open to new ideas. The Step by Step philosophy maintains that adults must model the qualities that they seek to develop in young children: creative thinking, problem-solving, lifelong learning, respectfulness of diversity, and teamwork.

## Child/Staff Ratios

The caregiver must be able to focus on each child as an individual; she must have the time to talk with him, encourage his activities, respond to the particular needs of his temperament, prevent a difficult or dangerous situation before it develops, know his family's preferences and expectations, and be familiar with the family's ethnic and religious traditions. This list does not even mention the many daily routines, such as feeding and diapering, which take longer for infants and toddlers than routines for older children.

Attempting to provide individualized, child-centered learning for infants and toddlers with insufficient staff leaves teachers feeling frustrated because they are so involved in basic routines that they have little opportunity to follow children's development. Under such circumstances, caregivers have little sense of involvement with that development. Yet research shows that the teacher's sense of purpose and enthusiasm are key factors in high quality child care and healthy development.

Some programs operate under the misguided assumption that they can "manage" larger child/staff ratios by clustering infants and toddlers into group activities. Although developmentally appropriate for older preschool children, group activities are inappropriate for younger ones. Such practice is not in the best interest of the children.

Research shows that children in programs with low child/staff ratios do better on developmental tests than do children in programs with higher ratios. Recommended child/staff ratios according to Head Start Performance Standards are 4 to 1 for infants and Toddlers. However, some experts argue for a smaller ratio for young and mobile infants (birth to 18 months): a ratio of 3 to 1

Because infant and toddler programs tend to have a high rate of absenteeism due to sickness, particularly among the infants, some programs have an *enrollment* child/staff ratio of 4 to 1, although the daily *operating* ratio is usually 3 to 1. Each state and local childcare agency has developed policies and guidelines that should be followed by participating childcare providers.

## Group Size

Many of the same factors that suggest low child/staff ratios also dictate small group sizes. Again, research shows that group size is just as important, and possibly more important, than child/staff ratio (Ruopp et al., 1979). It is a mistake to have many infants and toddlers and a large number of teachers in one very large room. The ratio might be correct, but the size of the group is too large.

Adults often react negatively to what they perceive as a large, noisy crowd. Young children tend to be even more negatively affected by noisy and chaotic conditions. (Chapters 2 and 3 summarized recent research showing the wide variations in children's "reactivity," their ability to adapt to lots of sensory stimulation.) Some infants' temperaments are such that they are impelled to "tune out" noisy environments. Consequently, these infants no longer relate to others. Many young children who behave well in individual or small group settings have substantially greater difficulty exercising self-control skills in a large group, since there are more distractions.

Caregivers must maintain both low child/staff ratios and small group sizes to optimize learning. Head Start Programs limit group size for infants and toddlers to no more than 8 children. Other experts have recommended the following group sizes:

- For young infants (birth to 8 months):     6 children per room
- For mobile infants (8 to 18 months):     9 children per room
- For toddlers (18 to 36 months):     12 children per room

## Continuity of Care

### A Primary Caregiver

Young children need to know that they can expect to have time with their unhurried teacher in a small group of children. Without it, the child loses the sense of attachment, of wanting to show or do something with someone whose interest or approval matters to him. Similarly, when parents can relate to the same person over an extended period of time, the bond between the caregiver and family becomes stronger. For these reasons, it is important to assign a particular person as the "primary caregiver" for each child. Assignments should be made carefully, after seeing which adults and children do best together. *The assignment of a primary caregiver does not mean that another caregiver will never attend to a child when the primary caregiver is busy.* These are general guidelines; common sense and flexibility should prevail at all times.

## Low Staff Turnover

Caregivers should spend most of the day with their assigned children, rather than rotating assignments. They should be paid a reasonable salary and receive benefits. It is also the responsibility of the program administration to make staff feel valued and appreciated through compensations other than financial rewards. Administrators can show staff that they are valued in many ways: training opportunities, memberships in professional associations, subscriptions to educational journals, gifts of early childhood textbooks or other literature, certificates of participation for completed training, opportunities for advancement, opportunities to make presentations at staff meetings, recognition for a job well-done.

If caregivers are enthusiastic about their assignments and feel a sense of accomplishment, they are likely to have low rates of absenteeism and remain in the job for a long time.

## Moving With the Children From Year to Year

The practice of having teachers and children stay together for several years is exemplary. Because learning occurs simultaneously with emotional attachment, it is best for infants and toddlers to have one primary caregiver throughout the first three years of life. According to this practice, a caregiver is assigned to a group of three young infants and stays with them through the mobile infant and toddler stages until they are three years old, whereupon she is assigned to a new group of young infants.

This practice fosters strong attachments and benefits the children by giving them caregivers who know them and their parents well. It also gives the caregiver a changing curriculum from year to year.

## *Staff Training and Education*

Caregivers need a solid educational background in theory as well as a practicum experience. Like the children in the program, caregivers should strive to be lifelong learners. Caregiver training should be ongoing since the process of learning about children and their families is a continuing one.

## Theoretical Background

All those who teach and care for infants and toddlers should have a theoretical background in early child development, child health and nutrition, and family studies, and some training in self-awareness. A broad theoretical background enables caregivers and teachers to be sensitive to the needs of the children and families they serve. It serves as an intellectual reference for the observed behavior of children and the application of knowledge to these observations.

## Practical Experience

Theory only comes alive as students apply it towards real children. Theoretical training should be accompanied by a college or university-supervised practicum or internship in one or more infant or toddler classrooms over three or four months. A practicum in a classroom of three- to five-year-olds is inadequate practical experience for infant and toddler caregivers because the methods of teaching are very different. The practicum should also include significant experience working with parents.

## Experience Teaching Children With Special Needs

As education becomes more inclusive, children with learning, physical, and developmental disabilities are increasingly cared for alongside children who are developing typically. Caregivers must broaden both their theoretical and practical background to include experience with non-typically developing children. The experience often provides strategies that improve the caregiver's skills with all children, regardless of their ability level.

Although inclusive classrooms are not appropriate for all children with special needs, many benefit from a "mainstream" setting. Very young children are among those who benefit greatly, especially if the alternative specialized care takes place in a residential setting, where the children are separated from family and other typically developing youngsters. Every practicum should include a rotation in a classroom that includes children with special needs so that teachers will feel that they are adequately prepared to serve them better.

## Ongoing Training

Infant and toddler caregivers need continuing training, just as doctors need to keep up with the latest research and treatments. Not only will they learn about new information or approaches to their work, but their individual and group morale will be higher and they will be more willing to try to new methods. A director's budget should include funds for professional development for individual teachers or groups of teachers.

Just as children learn based on their interests, developmental levels, individual needs, and strengths, so do teachers. A teacher may seek additional training for many reasons: the needs of one child or family in her care, an intellectual interest, or the requirements of professional advancement. Training should be available to each caregiver, regardless of motivation. The supervisor might assess the needs of the teaching team and determine that all staff or a group of staff will benefit from shared training. Alternatively, one staff member may receive specialized, individual training.

Suggested topics for ongoing training include the following:

- Involving families as partners in the program
- Developmental stages of infants and toddlers
- Observation techniques
- Health and safety practices
- Serving children with disabilities
- Cultural diversity
- Outdoor play activities
- The learning environment for infants and toddlers
- Recent research on the brain and infant learning

## Professional Development Day

As an incentive for building staff professionalism and instilling a sense of teamwork, at least one day per year should be dedicated to professional development. It could include any of the following experiences: a visit to a program with a different philosophy, attendance at a professional conference, a visit to a school that integrates children with special needs in classrooms with typically developing children, a visit to an institution with specialized services for children with special needs, a day in the classroom of a mentor teacher, or attendance at a seminar or lecture at a pedagogic institution.

The caregiver should prepare for the visit by writing out a set of objectives that she plans to accomplish or questions she wants answered during the visit. The caregiver should make a presentation of what she has learned at a subsequent staff meeting. In this way the experience extends to the entire staff and individual staff begin to develop a network of resources among themselves. Their professional regard for each other's experiences and strengths is also enhanced.

## Staff Orientation

All Step by Step staff at each site need to be fully informed about the program philosophy and committed to its principles. In-depth orientation should be required for all new staff at the time they join the program. Orientation review sessions should be required for all staff at the beginning of each year. The initial orientation sessions should include the following topics:

- Introduction to all staff
- Tour of the facility
- Step by Step program philosophy
- Basic program concepts: individualized learning, parent involvement, working in teams, developing secure attachments to children, developmentally appropriate practice, learning through play, and so forth
- Role of each staff member on the team, from top administrator to lowest level support person
- Arrangement of the learning environment, indoor and outdoors
- Confidentiality, health, safety, and emergency procedures
- Staff evaluation
- Program resources, internal and external
- Public relations information

# Guidance From Supervisory Staff

Caregivers have a continuing need to discuss their performance with a supervisor or another professional who can help them reflect on their relationships with the children, parents, and other staff.

## Helping Teachers Become More Self-aware

Teachers and caregivers bring feelings and memories of their own childhood experiences into the classroom. Those memories and experiences are very subjective and can powerfully influence their perceptions and behaviors.

Becoming aware of one's own prejudices and preferences is an ongoing process. As a starting point, a supervisor can use the following simple exercise at a staff meeting to raise self-awareness within teachers:

> *A group leader asks the teachers to think of a child that they find appealing and write down the child's qualities. The leader gathers the lists and copies them onto a large piece of paper. She then asks the group to think of a child whose behavior is annoying. Again, she gathers the lists and writes them in a column opposite the pleasant behaviors. What the group discovers is that the same qualities appear in both columns. Feisty behavior may be appealing to some and equally unappealing to another. Similarly, compliant behavior is both appealing and unappealing to different teachers.*

This discovery can be used as the basis for discussion and self-examination.

A caregiver must become aware of the behaviors that she admires and dislikes; she must recognize her tolerances, prejudices, and personal habits that influence her vision of the children in her care. Caregivers also need to understand and respect ethnic, language, and religious diversity, and not assume that individuals from differing backgrounds share the same traditions or values.

Honest self-examination is the first step to understanding and appreciating differing backgrounds, values, and temperaments. When a caregiver can discuss her feelings confidentially with a supervisor, they can work together to think through problem situations and develop strategies to cope with them.

## Community Resources and Professionals

Professionals in the fields of psychology, child development, or mental health can be called on to facilitate self-awareness among staff members. Outside professionals can observe the dynamics within the center or within particular classrooms and offer advice. For example, staff might be concerned about an eighteen-month-old's highly aggressive behavior and unwillingness to accept the caregivers' suggestions. The parents may also seem unwilling to accept or respond to caregivers' suggestions. An outside professional can observe the child carefully, perhaps work directly with the child, meet with the parents, and offer the staff constructive interventions. This kind of outside assistance can turn a potentially explosive situation into a successful learning experience for everyone.

## Team Building

A center for infants and toddlers that successfully provides a high-quality program is characterized by a well-trained staff functioning as a team. Teams serve as evolving support networks that change and adapt with the needs of the child. Parents, primary caregivers, support staff, and administrative staff make up the team that collectively provides for the growth and development of each child. When parents and caregivers see themselves as a team working together to do the best for the children in their care, each child benefits. Strong teams are characterized by:

- A shared vision
- Interdependence
- Commitment
- Accountability

The team works with families to develop a shared vision. Together they ask questions such as: "What do we want for our children?" and "What is best for the infants and toddlers in our care?" Collaborating to establish goals creates interdependence among team members. They learn to appreciate each other's unique talents and contributions. Problems become less confounding and easier to solve when many points of view are brought together.

Multiple perspectives provide a more complete understanding of a situation than any single individual's point of view. Team work is based on an intentional commitment to a shared goal. When that goal is high-quality care for infants and toddlers, the caregiving team combines talents and knowledge to be effective. Clearly defined roles allow for responsible team decisions and actions. Clear lines of responsibility must be developed and understood by the caregiving team if it is to function smoothly. Teams should meet weekly to plan daily schedules, make necessary adaptations for individual needs, and plan times for systematic observation of children. (Regular communication with parents keeps caregivers alert to children's changing needs.) Weekly planning defines the tasks to be accomplished and assigns responsibility for each task.

Caregivers and parents share the responsibility for developing collaborative relationships. Good relationships are built on communication, mutual respect, acceptance of differences, and the best interests of the child. As people work towards a common goal, attitudes change and understanding develops. Caregivers and parents also learn new skills and behaviors. Families benefit in many ways from being part of a strong team as they:

- Develop a personal commitment to the program
- View their child as an individual in relationship to others
- Learn about infant and child development
- Come to know the caregivers as individuals

239

- Acquire skills and learn activities they can do at home with their infant or toddler
- Become acquainted with other families with young children and have the opportunity to develop long-lasting friendships

Caregivers and staff also benefit from being part of a strong team as they:

- Spend more time with individual infants and toddlers
- Learn how parents interact with their infants and toddlers
- Learn new problem-solving strategies for scheduling and routines
- Increase awareness of diverse cultural child rearing practices
- Come to appreciate the varied skills, talents, and ways of loving their babies that families bring

## Staff Evaluation

Each teacher's work should be reviewed on a regular basis, at least once a year and preferably every six months. Evaluation should be a constructive process, supportive of the needs and strengths of the person being evaluated. It should not be a critical process, punitive or threatening. The person being evaluated should be completely informed about the process. If evaluation is to be constructive, a reciprocity between the person being evaluated and the supervisor is required. The person to be evaluated participates in the process in the following ways:

- Helps determine the standards against which she will be evaluated
- Understands the entire process—the form, the time frame, the consequences of the evaluation
- Has an opportunity to respond to the performance review either orally or in writing

The caregiver and supervisor should work together to set performance goals and objectives against which the caregiver will be evaluated. The caregiver then understands that she is accountable for meeting these agreed-upon goals and objectives. These goals and objectives must be viewed in the larger context of the program. If the program promotes partnerships with parents, then a caregiver must be able to demonstrate ways in which she has realized this objective in her work. She must set measurable objectives for herself: for example, "I will make at least one home visit semiannually."

The results of the evaluation should be discussed with the caregiver at a scheduled meeting. They should be framed in a positive manner, recognizing efforts to improve performance, successes where they occur, and opportunities for future growth. At the end of the review, new objectives are jointly set for future work. The process becomes a cycle of setting measurable goals, reviewing performance against them, and reestablishing new goals. Supervisory and administrative staff should also go through the same process of goal setting, monitoring against goals, and evaluation of outcomes. (It is important to include parents in the general review process; their input is valuable to assessment of staff performance.)

There are many less formal evaluation techniques that caregivers can use to improve their performance, including:

- Keeping a journal to analyze problems and successes
- Taking turns with other caregivers to observe interactions with children or families, using an observation checklist
- Taking turns videotaping each other during routines and interactions with children

All staff want to know how well they are doing and what they could be doing better. Regular formal and informal evaluation makes this possible and is fundamental to any professional person's career training and development.

## Program Evaluation

An effective approach to improving individual and collective staff performance is to see it in the context of the whole program. A worker has an increased incentive to do a good job when he understands the importance of his contribution to the entire program. A program evaluation with full staff participation is a key activity of any organization of quality. The first step in the process is an evaluation of the program by the immediate staff with input from the Board of Directors, the Parent Advisory Committee, and perhaps interested members of the community. (Input can also be sought by a group outside the program with a view toward objectivity.)

A program evaluation provides an opportunity to take stock of the overall performance by looking at achievements in each segment of activity. There are two types of evaluation: (1) *process* evaluation reviews how the program is serving children and their families and (2) *outcome* or *impact* evaluation views performance from the vantage of measurable results. Because the process evaluation focuses on program improvement, it is more useful for purposes here.

The first step in any type of evaluation is to specify its purpose and how the information will be used. This step will determine the areas of inquiry and the best respondents for providing information. The program director should appoint an Evaluation Committee to carry out this initial task. The Committee should have representatives from all participants and staff levels, including the director, a caregiver, a parent, and a board member. The Evaluation Committee should begin by determining the broad standard (such as a mission statement or philosophy) against which the program will be evaluated. Program areas to be examined usually include the following:

- Services to children
- Administration
- Family involvement
- Community involvement
- Learning environment
- Staff development
- Staffing
- Health and safety

The evaluation will point out program strengths as well as specific issues or weaknesses that need correction or improvement. If the program is unable to resolve some of the improvements with in-house expertise, it may be appropriate to contact outside specialists for advice.

## Process Evaluation

The Evaluation Committee should tailor specific questions to define the nature of the services offered and the concerns voiced by staff and parents. Some of the inquiries will seek irrefutable factual information. Other questions will be more subjective in nature: "In what ways do we think we could improve the care to infants?" Responses to these questions are subjective, but provide extremely useful insights when the respondents are experienced and knowledgeable. Both types of inquiries are useful and lead to an understanding of the actual situation and how it can be improved. Examples of both types of process evaluation questions are listed below.

> ***Factual Questions*** How many children does the program serve? How many families have been visited at home? How many children are in each classroom? How many staff are serving the children? What is the child/staff ratio? What is the staff absentee rate? What is the child absentee rate? What is the staff turnover rate? How many hours of staff training do we offer? Have we identified children with special needs? How many children with special needs do we serve? What percentage of staff are: very satisfied/satisfied/not very satisfied/dissatisfied with their work? What is the incidence of illness at the center?

> ***Subjective Questions*** How effectively does the program serve children in each of the developmental areas of learning: emotional, social, language, cognitive, physical? In what ways are staff putting into practice the program philosophy: learning through play, individualized teaching, family involvement, choice, developmentally appropriate practices, cultural diversity? How is the environment conducive to learning? How can it be improved? What are the program's major accomplishments? What are the major areas for improvement? How can the program more effectively serve children with disabilities? How have staff

been rewarded for accomplishments? What are the areas of staff satisfaction and dissatisfaction? What is being done about complaints or concerns? How can communication with parents be improved?

The evaluation findings should be available to all staff. Recommendations for sharing successful practices among staff should be a part of the report as well as recommendations for improving practices. The final step of the evaluation process is to set a work plan and time line to accomplish the proposed recommendations.

## Outcome Evaluation

An outcome evaluation systematically examines how well children and their families have been served by the program. It can assess their status immediately after the program (or some component of the program) is completed, or, it may take place some time later.

An outcome evaluation usually includes questions like these:

- What percentage of parents are satisfied with the program?
  √ Highly satisfied?
  √ Mostly satisfied?

- What percentage of children are progressing at developmentally appropriate rates?
  √ By what measures?

- What percentage of children are ready for a three- to five-year-old preschool program?
  √ By what assessment?

## *Conclusion*

The program for infants and toddlers that strives to constantly maintain and improve its quality has at its center a team that works together and always listens and learns from children, parents, and each other.

# REFERENCES

## CHAPTER 1

Bredekamp, S., & Copple, C. (Eds.) (1997). *Developmentally appropriate practice in early childhood programs.* Washington, DC: NAEYC.

Brooks, J., & M. (1993). *In search of understanding: The case for constructivist classrooms.* Alexandria, VA: Association for Supervision and Curriculum Development.

Frost, J., & Jacobs, P. (1995). Play deprivation: A factor in juvenile violence. *Dimensions of Early Childhood, 23*(3), 14-39.

Johnson, J.E., Christie, J.F., & Yawkey, T.D. (1987). *Play and early childhood development.* Glenview: Scott, Foresman, and Company.

Seefeldt, C., & Barbour, N. (1994). *Early childhood education: An introduction.* New York: MacMillan.


## CHAPTER 2

Ainsworth, M.D.S. (1967). *Infancy in Uganda: Infant care and the growth of love.* Baltimore, MD: Johns Hopkins University Press.

Ainsworth, M.D.S., Blehar, M.D., Waters, E., & Wall, S. (1978). *Patterns of Attachment: A psychological study of the strange situation.* Hillsdale, NJ: Erlbaum Press.

Alliance to End Childhood Lead Poisoning. (2000). *About Lead Poisoning.* www.aeclp.org.

Brazelton, T.B., Tronick, E., Adamson, L., Als, H., & Wise, S. (1975). Early mother-infant reciprocity. *Parent-infant interaction.* CIBA Foundation Symposium 33. New York and Amsterdam: Elsevier.

Brazelton, T.B., & Cramer, B.G. (1990). *The earliest relationship.* Reading, MA: Addison-Wesley Publishing.

Busch-Rossnagel, N.A. (1997). Mastery motivation in toddlers. *Infants and Young Children, 9*(4), 1-11.

Chang, H.N. with Pulido, D. (1994). The critical importance of cultural and linguistic continuity for infants and toddlers. *Zero to Three, 15*(2), 13-16.

Chasnoff, I.J., Griffith, D.R., Freier, C., & Murray, J. (1992). Cocaine/polydrug use and pregnancy: Two-year follow-up. *Pediatrics, 89,* 284-289.

Chen, L. (1983). Diarrhea and malnutrition. In L. Chen & N. Scrimshaw (Eds.), *Energy intake and activity.* (pp. 3-19). New York: Plenum Publishing.

Chugani, H., Phelps, M.E., & Mazziotta, J. C. (1987). Positron emission tomography study of human brain functional development. *Annals of Neurology,* 22(4), 495.

Cunningham, A.S., Jelliffe, D.B., & Jelliffe, E.F.P. (1991). Breast-feeding and health in the 1980's. A global epidemiologic review. *The Journal of Pediatrics, 118*(5), 659-666.

Di Pietro, J. (1997, April). *Maternal affect and fetal neurobehavioral development.* Paper presented at the meeting of the Society for Research in Child Development, Washington, DC.

Drotar, D. Pallotta, J., & Eckerle, D. (1994). A prospective study of family environments of children hospitalized for nonorganic failure-to-thrive. *Developmental and Behavioral Pediatrics, 15,* 78-85.

Eimas, P.O., Siqueland, E.R., Jusczyk, P., & Vigonto, J. (1971). Speech perception in infants. *Science, 171,* 303-306.

Erickson, M.F., & Pianta, R.C. (1989). New lunchbox, old feelings: What kids bring to school. *Early Education and Development, 1*(1), 40.

Erikson, Erik H. (1950). *Childhood and society.* New York: W. W. Norton & Co.

Espinosa, M.P., Sigman, M.D., Neumann, C.G., Bwibo, N.O., & McDonald, M.A. (1992). Playground behaviors of school-age children in relation to nutrition, schooling and family characteristics. *Developmental Psychology, 28,* 1188-1195.

Far West Laboratory and the California Department of Education. (1995). Module IV: Culture, Family, and Providers. *The program for infant/toddler caregivers.* Sacramento, CA: California Department of Education.

Fernald, A., Taeschner, T., Dunn, J., Papousek, M., de Boysson-Bardies, B., & Fukui, I. (1989). A cross-language study of prosodic modifications in mothers' and fathers' speech to preverbal infants. *Journal of Child Language, 16,* 477-501.

Fox, N.A. (1997, April). Attachment in infants and adults: A link between the two? Paper presented at the meeting of the Sociey for Research in Child Development. Washington, DC.

Greenough, W.T. (1987). Experience effects on the developing and the mature brain: Dendritic branching and synaptogenesis. In *Prenatal development: A psychobiological perspective* (pp. 195-221). New York: Academic Press.

Gunnar, M.R., Brodersen, L., Krueger, K., & Rigatuso, R. (1996). Dampening of behavioral and adrenocortical reactivity during early infancy: Normative changes and individual differences. *Child Development, 67,* 877-889.

Huttenlocher, P.R. (1994). Synaptogenesis, synapse elimination, and neural plasticity in human cerebral cortex. In C.A. Nelson (Ed.), *Threats to optimal development: Integrating biological, psychological and social risk factors* (pp. 35-54). The Minnesota Symposia in Child Psychology, 27.

Jusczyk, P., Friederici, A., Wessels, J., Svenkerud, V., & Jusczyk, A. (1993). *Journal of Memory and Language, 32*(402).

Kagan, J., Reznick, J.S., & Snidman, N. (1987). The physiology and psychology of behavioral inhibition in children. *Child Development, 58,* 1459-1473.

Klein, P.S. (1996). *Early intervention: Cross-cultural experiences with a mediational approach.* New York and London: Garland Publishing.

Klinnert, M.D., Emde, R.N., Butterfield, P., & Campos, J.J. (1986). Social referencing: The infant's use of emotional signals from a friendly adult with mother present. *Developmental Psychology, 22*(4), 427-432.

Lally, J.R. (1995). The impact of child care policies and practices on infant/toddler identity formation. *Young Children, 51*(1), 58-67.

Lewis, M., Sullivan, M.W., Stanger, C., & Weiss, M. (1989). Self development and self-conscious emotions. *Child Development, 60,* 146-156.

Lieberman, A.F. (1993). *The emotional life of the toddler.* New York: Free Press.

Lucas, A. (1992). *Dunn Nutrition Unit.* Cambridge, England: Cambridge University.

Mahler, M.S., Pine, F., & Bergman, A. (1975). *The psychological birth of the human infant.* New York, NY: Basic Books.

Mayes, L.C., Bornstein, M.H., Chawarska, K., Haynes, O.M., & Granger, R.H. (1996). Impaired regulation of arousal in 3-month-old infants exposed prenatally to cocaine and other drugs. *Development and Psychopathology, 8,* 29-42.

McEwen, B.S. (1992, April). Hormones and brain development. Address to the American Health Foundation, Washington, DC.

Miller, D.F. (1989). *First steps toward cultural difference: Socialization in infant/toddler day care*. Washington, DC: Child Welfare League of America.

Morisset, C.E. (1991). What's it mean to share a story? *Zero to Three, 12*(1), 10-14.

Nachmias, M., Gunnar, M., Mangelsdorf, S., Parritz, R., & Buss, K. (1996). Behavioral inhibition and stress reactivity: Moderating role of attachment security. *Child Development, 67,* 508-522.

National Academy of Sciences. (1995). Seventh Annual Symposium on Frontiers of Science. *Science, 270,* 1294.

Needleman, H.L., Schell, A., Bellinger, D., Leviton, A., & Allred, E.N. (1990). Long term effects of childhood exposure to lead at low dose: An eleven-year follow-up report. *New England Journal of Medicine, 321,* 83-88.

Nelson, K. (1996). *Language in cognitive development: Emergence of the mediated mind.* New York: Cambridge University Press.

Olson, H.C., Sampson, P.D., Barr, H., Streissguth, A.P., & Bookstein, F.L. (1992). Prenatal exposure to alcohol and school problems in late childhood: A longitudinal prospective study. *Development and Psychopathology, 4*(3), 341-359.

Phillips, C.B. (1988). Nurturing diversity of today's children and tomorrow's leaders. *Young Children, 43*(2), 42-47.

Piaget, J. (1952). *The origins of intelligence in children.* New York: International Universities Press.

Pollitt, E. (1996). A reconceptualization of the effects of undernutrition on children's biological, psychosocial, and behavioral development. *Social Policy Report, 10*(5).

Rizzo, T.A., Metzger, B.E., Dooley, S.L., & Cho, N.H. (1997). Early malnutrition and child neurobehavioral development: Insights from the study of children of diabetic mothers. *Child Development, 68*(1), 26-38.

Saffran, J.R., Aslin, R.N., & Newport, E.L. (1996). Statistical learning by 8-month-old infants. *Science, 274,* 1926-1928.

Stroufe, L.A., & Waters, E. (1977). Attachment as an organizational construct. *Child Development, 48,* 1184-1199.

Steissguth, A.P., Martin, DC, & Barr, H.M. (1989). IQ at age 4 in relation to maternal alcohol use and smoking during pregnancy. *Developmental Psychology, 25,* 3-11.

Stern, D. (1985). *The interpersonal world of the infant.* New York: Basic Books.

Thomas, A., & Chess, S. (1977). *Temperament and development.* New York: Brunner/Mazel.

Tronick, E., Als, H., Adamson, L., Wise, S., & Brazelton, T.B. (1978). The infant's response to entrapment between contradictory messages in face-to-face interaction. *Journal of Child Psychiatry, 17,* 1-13.

Vygotsky, L.S. (1986). *Thought and language.* Cambridge, MA: MIT Press. (First published 1934).

Weissbourd, R. (1996). *The Vulnerable Child: What really hurts America's children and what we can do about it.* Reading, MA: Addison-Wesley Publishing.

Whitehurst, G.J., Falco, F.L., Lonigan, C.J., Fischel, J.E., & Caulfield, M. (1988). Accelerating language development through picture book reading. *Developmental Psychology, 24,* 552-559.

Yarrow, L.J. (1981, March). Beyond cognition: The development of mastery motivation. *Zero to Three, 1*(3), 1-5.

Yogman, M.W. (1982). Development of the father-infant relationship. In Fitzgerald, H., Lester, B., and Yogman, M.W. (Eds.), *Theory and research in behavioral pediatrics* (pp. 221-279). New York: Plenum Press.

Zahn-Waxler, C., & Radke-Yarrow, M. (1982). The development of altruism: Alternative research strategies. In Eisenberg, N. (Ed.), *Development of social behavior.* New York: Academic Press.

Zuckerman, B., & Brown, E. (1993). Maternal substance abuse and infant development. In Zeanah, C.H., Jr. (Ed.), *Handbook of infant mental health* (pp. 143-158). New York: Guilford Press.

## CHAPTER 3

Beckwith, L. (1990). Adaptive and maladaptive parenting–Implications for intervention. In Meisels, S.J., & Shonkoff, J.P. (Eds.), *Handbook of early childhood intervention* (pp. 53-77). New York: Cambridge University Press.

Belsky, J., & Isabella, R.A. (1988). Maternal, infant, and social-contextual determinants of attachment security. In Belsky, J., & Nezworski, T. (Eds.), *Clinical implications of attachment* (pp. 41-94). Hillsdale, NJ: Erlbaum Press.

Belsky, J., & Pensky, E. (1988). Developmental history, personality, and family relationships: Toward an emergent family system. In Hinde, R.A., & Stevenson-Hinde, J. (Eds.). *Relationships within families: Mutual influences* (pp. 193-217). New York: Oxford University Press.

Caughy, M.O., DiPietro, J.A., & Strobino, D.M. (1994). Day-care participation as a protective factor in the cognitive development of low-income children. *Child Development, 65,* 457-471.

Chasnoff, I., Griffith, D., Frier, C., & Murray, J. (1992). Cocaine/polydrug use in pregnancy: Two-year follow-up. *Pediatrics 89(2),* 284-289.

Cost, Quality, & Child Outcomes Study Team. (1995). *Cost, quality, and child outcomes in child care centers: Public report.* Denver: Economics Department, University of Colorado at Denver.

Duncan, G.J., Brooks-Gunn, J., & Klebanov, P.K. (1994). Economic deprivation and early childhood development. *Child Development, 65(2),* 296-318.

Dunst, C.J., & Trivette, C.M. (1990). Assessment of social support in early intervention programs. In Meisels, S.J., & Shonkoff, J.P., *Handbook of early childhood intervention* (pp. 326-349). New York: Cambridge University Press.

Elder, G.H., Jr. (1974). *Children of the Great Depression: Social change in life experience.* Chicago, University of Chicago Press.

Galinsky, E., Bond, J.T., & Friedman, D.E. (1993). *Highlights: The national study of the changing workforce.* New York: Families and Work Institute.

Greenspan, S.I., & Wieder, S. (1993). Regulatory disorders. In Zeanah, C.H., Jr. (Ed.), *Handbook of infant mental health.* New York: Guilford Press.

Halpern, R. (1993). Poverty and infant development. In Zeanah, C.H., Jr. (Ed.). *Handbook of infant mental health* (pp. 73-86). New York: Guilford Press.

Hayes, C.D., Palmer, J.L., & Zaslow, M.J. (Eds.). (1990). *Who cares for America's children? Child care policy for the 1990's.* Washington, DC: National Academy Press.

Howes, C., Smith, E., & Galinsky, E. (1995). *The Florida child care quality improvement study.* New York: Families and Work Institute.

Lally, J.R., Mangione, P.L., Honig, A.S., & Wittmer, D.S. (1988). More pride, less delinquency: Findings from the ten-year follow-up study of the Syracuse. University Family Development Research Program. *Zero to Three, 3*(4), 13-18.

Lewis, M., & Rosenblum, L. (Eds.) (1974). *The effect of the infant on its caregiver.* New York: John Wiley.

National Center for Clinical Infant Programs (NCCIP). (1988). *Infants, families, and child care: Toward a research agenda.* Washington, DC: National Center/Zero to Three.

National Child Care Staffing Study. (1989). *Who cares? Child care teachers and the quality of care in America.* Oakland, CA: Child Care Employee Project.

Osofsky, J.D. (1997). *Children in a violent society.* New York: Guilford Press.

Pruett, K. (1987). *The nurturing father.* New York, NY: Warner Books.

Ramey, C.T., Bryant, D.M., Sparling, J.J., & Wasik, B. H. (1985). Project CARE: A comparison of two early intervention strategies to prevent retarded development. *Topics in Early Childhood Special Education, 1*, 1-9.

Ruopp, R., Travers, J., Glantz, F., & Coelen, C. (1979). *Children at the center: Summary findings and their implications. Final Report of the National Day Care Study, Volume 1.* Cambridge, MA: Abt Associates.

Rutter, M. (1979). Protective factors in children's responses to stress and disadvantage. In Kent, M.W., & Rolf, J.E. (Eds.), *Primary prevention of psychopathology: Vol. 3 – Social competence in children* (pp. 49-74). Hanover, NH: University Press of New England.

Sameroff, A.J., & Fiesse, B.H. (1990). Transactional regulation and early intervention. In Meisels, S.J., & Shonkoff, J.P. (Eds.), *Handbook of early childhood intervention* (pp. 119-149). New York: Cambridge University Press.

Sameroff, A.J., Seifer, R., Barocas, B., Zax, M., & Greenspan, S. (1987). IQ scores of 4-year-old children: Social-environmental risk factors. *Pediatrics 79*(3), 343-350.

Stern, D. (1985). *The interpersonal world of the infant.* New York: Basic Books.

Tinsley, B.J., & Parke, R.D. (1987). Grandparents as interactive and social support agents for families with young children. *International Journal of Aging and Human Development, 25*(4).

U.S. Department of Health and Human Services, National Institute for Child Health and Development (NICHD), Early Child Care Research Network. (1996, April). *Infant child care and attachment security: Results of the NICHD study of early child care.* Symposium conducted at the meeting of the International Conference on Infant Studies, Providence, RI.

Werner, E.E. (1982). *Vulnerable but invincible: A longitudinal study of resilient children and youth.* New York: McGraw Hill.

Yogman, M.W. (1982). Development of the father-infant relationship. In Fitzgerald, H., Lester, B., and Yogman, M.W. (Eds.), *Theory and research in behavioral pediatrics.* (pp. 221-279). New York: Plenum Press.


## CHAPTER 4

Erikson, Erik H. (1950). *Childhood and society.* New York: W. W. Norton Co.

Kostelnik, M. J., Stein, L.C., Whiren, A. P., & Soderman, A. K. 1993. *Guiding children's social development.* Albany, NY: Delmar Publishers.

Wilson, L. C., Douville-Watson, L., & Watson, M. A. (1995). *Infants and toddlers: Curriculum and teaching.* Albany, NY: Delmar Publishers.


## CHAPTER 5

Council for Early Childhood Professional Recognition. (1991). *CDA competency standards for infant/toddler caregivers in center-based programs.* Washington, DC: author.

Dodge, D. T., Dombro, A. L., & Koralek, D. G. (1991). *Caring for infants and toddlers, Vol. II.* Washington, DC: Teaching Strategies Incorporated.

Gonzalez-Mena, J., & Eyer, D. W. (1997). *Infants, toddlers and caregivers.* Mountain View, CA: Mayfield Publishing.

Kostelnik, M. J., Stein, L.C., Whiren, A. P. & Soderman, A. K. (1993). *Guiding children's social development.* Albany, NY: Delmar Publishers.

National Association for the Education of Young Children. (1996). Biters: Why they do it and what to do about it. *The early years are learning years.* Washington, DC: NAEYC Homepage, pubaff@naeyc.org.

Wilson, L. C., Douville-Watson, L., & Watson, M. A. (1995). *Infants and toddlers: Curriculum and teaching.* Albany, NY: Delmar Publishers.


**CHAPTER 6**

Bornstein, M. C. & Bornstein, H. G. (1995). Caregivers' responsiveness and cognitive development in infants and toddlers: Theory and research. In P. L. Mangione (Ed.). *Infant/ toddler caregiving: A guide to cognitive development and learning* (pp. 12-21). Sacramento, CA: California Department of Education.

Carew, J. V. Chan. I., & Halfar, C. (1976). *Observing intelligence in young children.* Englewood Cliffs, NJ: Prentice Hall.

Greenman, J., & Stonehouse, A. (1996). *Primetimes: A handbook for excellence in infant and toddler programs.* St. Paul, MN: Redleaf.

Honig, A.S. (1991). For babies to flourish. *Montessori LIFE, 3*(2), 7-10.


**CHAPTER 7**

Cawlfield, M. E. (1992). Velcro time: The language connection. *Young Children, 47*(4), 26-30.

Honig, A. S., & Brophy, H. E. (1996). *Talking with your baby: Family as the first school.* Syracuse, NY: Syracuse University Press.

Owens, R. E. (1996). *Language development.* (4th ed.) Boston, MA: Allyn and Bacon.

Klein, P. S. (1996). *Early Intervention: Cross-cultural experiences with a mediational approach.* New York and London: Garland Publishing.


**CHAPTER 8**

Furuno, S., O'Reilly, K. A., Inatsuka, T. T., Hosaka, C. M., & Falbey, B. Z. (1993). *Helping babies learn.* Tucson, AZ: Communication Skill Builders.

Greenspan, S. I. (1995). *The challenging child: Understanding, raising, and enjoying the five "difficult" types of children.* NY: Addison-Wesley Publishing.

Honig, A. S., & Lally, J. R. (1981). *Infant caregiving: A design for training.* Syracuse, NY: Syracuse University Press.

## CHAPTER 12

American Public Health Association & American Academy of Pediatrics. (1992). *Caring for our children: National health and safety performance standards–Guidelines for out-of-home child care programs.* Washington, DC: American Public Health Association.

American Red Cross. (1993). *Community first aid and safety.* Washington, DC: author.

Bronson, M.B. (1995). *The right stuff for children birth to 8: Selecting play materials to support development.* Washington, DC: National Association for the Education of Young Children.

Centers for Disease Control and Prevention. (1996) *The ABCs of Safe and Healthy Child Care.* (www.cdc.gov.).

Colorado Department of Education. (1994, November). *Quality standards for early childhood care and education services: A planning document.* Denver: author.

Lally, J.R., & Stewart, J. 1990. *Infant and toddler caregiving: A guide to setting up environments.* Sacramento, CA: California Department of Education.

National Association of State Boards of Education. Task Force on Early Childhood Education. 1988. *Right from the start.* Alexandria, VA: author.

Shapiro Kendrick, A., Kaufmann, R., & Messenger, K. (Eds.) (1991). *Healthy Young Children: A Manual for Programs.* Washington, DC: National Association for the Education of Young Children.

Starr, S.A. (1996, May/June). Breaking the chain: Handwashing and infections control. Early Childhood News. *The Journal of Professional Development, 8*(3).

Texas Department of Protective and Regulatory Services. (1995). *Day care center minimum standards and guidelines.* Austin, TX: author.

Torelli, L., & Durrett, C. (1996). *Landscapes for learning: Designing group care environments for infants, toddlers and two-year-olds.* Berkeley, CA: author.

## CHAPTER 13

American Public Health Association & American Academy of Pediatrics. (1992). *Caring for our children: National health and safety performance standards–Guidelines for out-of-home child care programs.* Washington, DC: American Public Health Association.

American Red Cross. (1993). *Community first aid and safety.* Washington, DC: author.


**CHAPTER 14**

American Public Health Association & American Academy of Pediatrics. (1992).
  *Caring for our children: National health and safety  performance standards–Guidelines
  for out-of-home child care programs.* Washington, DC: American Public Health
  Association.

Texas Department of Protective and Regulatory Services. (1995). *Day-care center minimum standards and guidelines.* Austin,TX: author.

U.S. Department of Agriculture and U.S. Department of Health and Human Services.
  (1985). *Nutrition and your health: Dietary guidelines for Americans.* (2nd Edition).
  Home and Garden Bulletin No. 232. Washington, DC: U.S. Government
  Printing Office.


**CHAPTER 16**

Fenichel, E. (Ed.) (1992). *Learning through supervision and mentorship:  A source book.*
  Washington, DC: Zero to Three.

Roupp, R., Bache, III, W.L., O'Neil, C., Singer, J., Irwin, N (ed.). (1979). *Children at the
  center: Summary findings and their implications.* Cambridge, MA: Abt books.

# Developmental Milestones of Children from Birth to Age 3

| | Interest in others | Self-awareness | Motor milestones and eye-hand skills |
|---|---|---|---|
| **The Early Months** (birth through 8 months) | • Newborns prefer the human face and human sound. Within the first 2 weeks, they recognize and prefer the sight, smell, and sound of the principal caregiver.<br>• Social smile and mutual gazing are evidence of early social interaction. Can initiate and terminate these interactions.<br>• Anticipates being lifted or fed and moves body to participate.<br>• Sees adults as objects of interest and novelty. Seeks out adults for play. Stretches arms to be taken. | • Sucks fingers or hand fortuitously.<br>• Observes own hands.<br>• Places hand up as an object comes close to the face as if to protect self.<br>• Looks to the place on body where being touched.<br>• Reaches for and grasps toys.<br>• Clasps hands together and fingers them.<br>• Tries to cause things to happen.<br>• Begins to distinguish friends from strangers. Shows preference for being held by familiar people. | • The young infant uses many complex reflexes: searches for something to suck; holds on when falling; turns head to avoid obstruction of breathing; avoids brightness, strong smells, and pain.<br>• Puts hand or object in mouth. Begins reaching toward interesting objects.<br>• Grasps, releases, regrasps, and releases object again.<br>• Lifts head. Holds head up. Sits up without support. Rolls over.<br>• Transfers and manipulates objects with hands. Crawls. |
| **Crawlers and Walkers** (8 to 18 months) | • Exhibits anxious behavior around unfamiliar adults.<br>• Enjoys exploring objects with another as the basis for establishing relationships.<br>• Gets others to do things for child's pleasure (wind up toys, read books, get dolls).<br>• Shows considerable interest in peers.<br>• Demonstrates intense attention to adult language.<br>• Models adult behaviors like vacuuming, setting table, putting on coat and carrying purse to "go work," using a telephone or another object as a telephone.<br>• Enacts simple dramatic play scenarios with others, like caring for dolls, acting like an animal, or riding in a car or train. | • Knows own name.<br>• Smiles or plays with self in mirror.<br>• Uses large and small muscles to explore confidently when a sense of security is offered by presence of caregiver. Frequently checks for caregiver's presence.<br>• Has heightened awareness of opportunities to make things happen, yet limited awareness of responsibility for own actions.<br>• Indicates strong sense of self through assertiveness. Directs actions of others (e.g., "Sit there!")<br>• Identifies one or more body parts.<br>• Begins to use *me, you, I.* | • Sits well in chairs.<br>• Pulls self up, stands holding furniture.<br>• Walks when led. Walks alone.<br>• Throws objects.<br>• Climbs stairs.<br>• Uses marker on paper.<br>• Stoops, trots, can walk backward a few steps. |
| **Toddlers and 2-Year-Olds** (18 months to 3 years) | • Shows increased awareness of being seen and evaluated by others.<br>• Sees others as a barrier to immediate gratification.<br>• Begins to realize others have rights and privileges.<br>• Gains greater enjoyment from peer play and joint exploration.<br>• Begins to see benefits of cooperation.<br>• Identifies self with children of same age of sex.<br>• Is more aware of the feelings of others.<br>• Exhibits more impulse control and self-regulation in relation to others.<br>• Enjoys small group activities.<br>• Acts out simple dramatic play themes with others ("You, baby; me, mommy"; going to the store, cooking dinner, preparing for a party.) | • Shows strong sense of self as an individual, as evidenced by "NO" to adult requests.<br>• Experiences self as a powerful, potent, creative doer. Explores everything.<br>• Becomes capable of self-evaluation and has beginning notions of self (good, bad, attractive, ugly).<br>• Makes attempts at self-regulation.<br>• Uses names of self and others.<br>• Identifies 6 or more body parts. | • Scribbles with marker or crayon.<br>• Walks up and down stairs. Can jump off one step.<br>• Kicks a ball.<br>• Stands on one foot.<br>• Threads beads.<br>• Draws a circle.<br>• Stands and walks on tiptoes.<br>• Walks up stairs one foot on each step.<br>• Handles scissors.<br>• Imitates a horizontal crayon stroke. |

Note: This list is not intended to be exhaustive. Many of the behaviors indicated here will happen earlier or later for individual infants. The chart suggests an approximate time when a behavior might appear, but it should not be rigidly interpreted.

Often, but not always, the behaviors appear in the order in which they emerge. Particularly for younger infants, the behaviors listed in one domain overlap considerably with several other developmental domains. Some behaviors are placed under more than one category to emphasize this interrelationship.

## Language development communication

- Cries to signal pain or distress.
- Smiles or vocalizes to initiate social contact.
- Responds to human voices. In the first month can distinguish familiar human voices from all other sounds. Gazes at faces.
- Uses vocal and nonvocal communication to express interest and exert influence.
- Babbles using all types of sounds. Engages in private conversations when alone.
- Combines babbles. Understands names of familiar people and objects. Laughs. Listens to conversations.
- By about 6 months, distinguishes sounds of home language from other speech.

- Uses eye contact to check back with primary caregiver.
- By about 8 months, turns to look at an object, like a ball, on hearing the word "ball" in the home language.
- Understands many more words than can say. Looks toward 20 or more objects when named.
- Creates long babbled sentences.
- Shakes head no. Says 2 or 3 clear words.
- Looks at picture books with interest, points to objects.
- Uses vocal signals other than crying to gain assistance.
- Begins to use *me, you, I.*

- Combines words.
- Listens to stories for a short while.
- Speaking vocabulary may reach 200 words.
- Develops fantasy in language. Begins to play pretend games.
- Defines use of many household items.
- Uses compound sentences.
- Uses adjectives and adverbs. Recounts events of the day.

## Physical, spatial, and temporal awareness

- Comforts self by sucking thumb or finding pacifier.
- Follows a slowly moving object with eyes.
- Recognizes expected patterns of objects in motion (such as arc, bounce, or slide).
- Reaches and grasps toys.
- Looks for dropped toy.
- Remembers intricate details of an object (such as a mobile) and shows signs of recognition on seeing the object again.
- Identifies objects from various viewpoints. Finds a toy hidden under a blanket when placed there while watching.
- Predicts a sequence of events after seeing the sequence a number of times.

- Tries to build with blocks.
- If toy is hidden under 1 of 3 cloths while child watches, looks under the right cloth for the toy.
- Persists in a search for a desired toy even when toy is hidden under distracting objects such as pillows.
- When chasing a ball that rolled under sofa and out the other side, will make a detour around sofa to get ball.
- Pushes foot into shoe, arm into sleeve.

- Identifies a familiar object by touch when placed in a bag with 2 other objects.
- Uses "tomorrow," "yesterday."
- Figures out which child is missing by looking at children who are present.
- Asserts independence: "Me do it."
- Puts on simple garments such as cap or slippers.

## Purposeful action and use of tools

- Observes own hands.
- Grasps rattle when hand and rattle are both in view.
- Hits or kicks an object to make a pleasing sight or sound continue.
- Tries to resume a knee ride by bouncing to get adult started again.

- When a toy winds down, continues the activity manually.
- Uses a stick as a tool to obtain a toy.
- When a music box winds down, searches for the key to wind it up again.
- Brings a stool to use for reaching for something.
- Pushes away someone or something not wanted.
- Creeps or walks to get something or avoid unpleasantness.
- Pushes foot into shoe, arm into sleeve.
- Partially feeds self with fingers or spoon.
- Handles cup well with minimal spilling.
- Handles spoon well for self-feeding.

- When playing with a ring-stacking toy, ignores any forms that have no hole. Stacks only rings or other objects with holes.
- Classifies, labels, and sorts objects by group (hard versus soft, large versus small).
- Helps dress and undress self.
- Uses objects as if they were something else (block, as car, big block as bus, box as house).

## Expression of feelings

- Expresses discomfort and comfort/pleasure unambiguously.
- Responds with more animation and pleasure to primary caregiver than to others.
- Can usually be comforted by familiar adult when distressed.
- Smiles and shows obvious pleasure in response to social stimulation. Very interested in people. Shows displeasure at loss of social contact.
- Laughs aloud (belly laugh).
- Shows displeasure or disappointment at loss of toy.
- Expresses several clearly differentiated emotions: pleasure, anger, anxiety or fear, sadness, joy, excitement, disappointment, exuberance.
- Reacts to strangers with soberness or anxiety.

- Actively shows affection for familiar person: hugs, smiles at, runs toward, leans against, and so forth.
- Shows anxiety at separation from primary caregiver.
- Shows anger focused on people or objects.
- Expresses negative feelings.
- Shows pride and pleasure in new accomplishments.
- Shows intense feelings for parents.
- Continues to show pleasure in mastery.
- Asserts self, indicating strong sense of self.

- Frequently displays aggressive feelings and behaviors.
- Exhibits contrasting states and mood shifts (stubborn versus compliant).
- Shows increased fearfulness (dark, monsters, etc.).
- Expresses emotions with increasing control.
- Aware of own feelings and those of others.
- Shows pride in creation and production.
- Verbalizes feelings more often. Expresses feelings in symbolic play.
- Shows empathic concern for others.

Source: Lally, J.R., Griffin, A., Fenichel, E., Segal, M., Szanton, E., & Weissbourd, B. (1995). Caring for Infants and Toddlers in Groups: Developmentally Appropriate Practice. Arlington, VA: ZERO TO THREE. Copyright 1995 by ZERO TO THREE. Reprinted with permission.

# Conversion Chart

| If you know... | you can find | if you multiply by |
| --- | --- | --- |
| 1 teaspoon | mililiters | 4.93 |
| 1 tablespoon | mililiters | 14.79 |
| 1 fluid ounce (fl. oz) | mililiters | 29.58 |
| 1 cup | liters | .24 |
| 1 pint | liters | .47 |
| 1 quart | liters | .95 |
| 1 gallon | liters | 3.79 |

## Temperature

To convert degrees Fahrenheit to degrees Celsius, subtract 32 and then multiply the answer by five ninths (.56).

To convert Celsius to Fahrenheit, multiply by nine fifths (1.8) and then add 32.

# Recommended Childhood Immunization Schedule
## Notes

[3]The 4th dose of DTaP (diphtheria and tetanus toxoids and acellular pertussis vaccine) may be administered as early as 12 months of age, provided 6 months have elapsed since the 3rd dose and the child is unlikely to return at age 15-18 months. Td (tetanus and diphtheria toxoids) is recommended at 11-12 years of age if at least 5 years have elapsed since the last dose of DTP, DTAP or DT. Subsequent routine Td boosters are recommended every 10 years.

[4]Three Haemophilus influenzae type b (Hib) conjugate vaccines are licensed for infant use. If PRP-OMP (PedvaxHIB) or ComVax [Merck]) is administered at 2 and 4 months of age, a dose at 6 months is not required. Because clinical studies in infants have demonstrated that using some combination products may induce a lower immune response to the Hib vaccine component, DTaP/Hib combination products should not be used for primary immunization in infants at 2, 4 or 6 months of age, unless FDA-approved for these ages.

[5]To eliminate the risk of vaccine-associated paralytic polio (VAPP), an all-IPV schedule is now recommended for routine childhood polio vaccination in the United States. All children should receive four doses of IPV at 2 months, 4 months, 6-18 months, and 4-6 years. OPV (if available) may be used only for the following special circumstances:
1. Mass vaccination campaigns to control outbreaks of paralytic polio.
2. Unvaccinated children who will be traveling in <4 weeks to areas where polio is endemic or epidemic.
3. Children of parents who do not accept the recommended number of vaccine injections. These children may receive OPV only for the third or fourth dose or both; in this situation, health-care providers should administer OPV only after discussing the risk for VAPP with parents or caregivers.
4. During the transition to an all-IPV schedule, recommendations for the use of remaining OPV supplies in physicians' offices and clinics have been issued by the American Academy of Pediatrics (see Pediatrics, December 1999).

[6]The 2nd dose of measles, mumps, and rubella (MMR) vaccine is recommended routinely at 4-6 years of age but may be administered during any visit, provided at least 4 weeks have elapsed since receipt of the 1st dose and that both doses are administered beginning at or after 12 months of age. Those who have not previously received the second dose should complete the schedule by the 11-12 year old visit.

[7]Varicella (Var) vaccine is recommended at any visit on or after the first birthday for susceptible children, i.e. those who lack a reliable history of chickenpox (as judged by a health care provider) and who have not been immunized. Susceptible persons 13 years of age or older should receive 2 doses, given at least 4 weeks apart.

[8]Hepatitis A (Hep A) is shaded to indicate its recommended use in selected states and/or regions; consult your local public health authority. (Also see MMWR Oct. 01, 1999/48(RR12); 1-37).

Source: Centers for Disease Control and Prevention (CDC)

# CREATING CHILD-CENTERED CLASSROOM SERIES

## CREATING CHILD-CENTERED CLASSROOMS: 3-5 YEAR OLDS

Helps teachers create active learning environments for preschool-age children, individualize teaching, and involve families in the program. Teachers learn observation techniques to teach to the strengths, interests, and needs of each child.

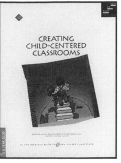

## CREATING CHILD-CENTERED MATERIALS FOR MATH AND SCIENCE

Assists educators in designing and making their own classroom materials for active exploration in math and science. Each activity includes a "home connection" that links the child's family to the classroom learning experiences. Easy-to-follow directions allow teachers to create activities from recycled and natural materials.

## CREATING CHILD-CENTERED CLASSROOMS: 6-7 YEAR OLDS

Provides teachers with lessons, suggestions for extending activities, assessment strategies and forms, thematic curriculum webs, and complete resource and reference lists. This volume presents four powerful themes that unify program concepts and goals: Communication, Caring, Community, and Connections.

## CREATING CHILD-CENTERED PROGRAMS FOR INFANTS AND TODDLERS

Provides the research base that supports the need for quality programs. It shows caregivers how to design a safe, healthy, and responsive environment for infants and toddlers; how to support young children's learning; and how to staff and evaluate a child-centered program for infants and toddlers.

## LEARNING ACTIVITIES FOR INFANTS AND TODDLERS: AN EASY GUIDE FOR EVERYDAY USE

Offers caregivers more than 100 hands-on, developmentally appropriate activities that caregivers can incorporate into the child's day. Each activity includes a purpose, list of materials, and simple steps for preparation. In addition, each activity provides a "home connection," to involve parents and extend the activity at home.

## CREATING INCLUSIVE CLASSROOMS

Provides the research base, practical methods and real-world case studies that guide and support teachers through issues such as family partnerships, IEP development, and adapting the classroom environment.

## CREATING CHILD-CENTERED CLASSROOMS: 8-10 YEAR OLDS

Presents a unique blend of current, exemplary educational practices and sound theory to address the educational needs of children in the later early childhood years. It addresses the content areas of mathematics, literacy, social studies, science, and the visual arts.

*For more information, contact:*

Children's Resources International
5039 Connecticut Ave., NW
Suite One
Washington, DC 20008
phone: 202-363-9002
fax: 202-363-9550
info@crinter.com

## EDUCATION AND THE CULTURE OF DEMOCRACY

Explains the link between democracy and early childhood practice. This book contends that there are subtle, yet effective teaching techniques that encourage democracy: choice, individualism, creativity, equality, respect for differences, and appreciation of individuals' needs while maintaining the balance for the greater good of the group.

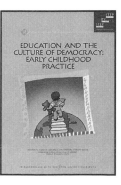